D1221319

13420

QL
776
C64

Cohen, Daniel
Talking with the
animals

Date Due

PLATTE COLLEGE RESOURCE CENTER
COLUMBUS, NEBRASKA

 PRINTED IN U.S.A.

Talking with the Animals

Daniel Cohen

———

TALKING WITH THE ANIMALS

Illustrated with photographs

DODD, MEAD & COMPANY
NEW YORK

ILLUSTRATION CREDITS

The photographs in this book are used by permission and through the courtesy of the following:

Bruce Frisch, page 127
Jim Kalett, pages 51, 54
Marineland of Florida, pages 109, 113, 117, 120, 121, 123
Milbourne Christopher Collection, pages 5, 7
National Geographic Society, pages 67, 73 by Alan Root;
    pages 80, 81 by Baron Hugo van Lawick
San Diego Zoo Photographs, pages 86, 89, 93; pages 33,
    43, 49, 64, 69 by Ron Garrison
Science Digest, pages 35, 38, 39
USDA Photographs, pages 18, 21
Diagram on page 19 by Jane O'Regan

To Jim, Carolyn, Ethan, and Olive

Contents

1

The Secret Languages

Not long ago, the people who lived in or near the jungles of the islands of Borneo and Sumatra held a very curious belief about the orangutan. The natives said that these great apes could talk as well as you and I. According to the story, the orangutans were capable of carrying on long and intelligent conversations with one another.

Outsiders were naturally skeptical about the orangutan's reputed ability to talk. Some French scientists asked the natives why no Frenchman had ever heard the apes conversing. The natives replied that the orangutans hid their ability to talk while outsiders were around. Why? Because the apes were afraid that if outsiders found out how smart apes really were they would be treated like the people of the islands. That meant they would be forced to work, pay taxes, and serve in the army.

Perhaps these East Indian natives were just making a bitter observation about how they themselves had been treated. But perhaps the story of the talking apes was meant to be literally true. Like all people who live close

1

to nature, the East Indian natives are keen observers of animal life. They have a high regard for animal intelligence and for the ability of animals to communicate with one another. The belief that animals have languages of their own is very ancient and very widespread.

For centuries man has been fascinated by the possibility that he could learn the secret language of the animals.

Earliest man was a hunter. His simple life was not so very different from that of the animals around him. Since he knew that men could talk with one another, he probably assumed that animals could do the same. The only problem was in understanding what the animals were saying to each other. Later, as man domesticated animals, he faced a more immediate and practical problem—getting the animals to understand what *he* said.

So the desire to "talk to the animals" has been with us for a long time.

Almost every society has its myths and legends about people who somehow obtained the ability of talking to animals. One of the great ancient myths of the Scandinavian people concerns the deeds of the hero Siegfried. In one of his exploits Siegfried kills a dragon named Fafnir. The hero cuts out the dragon's heart and roasts it over a fire. In order to see if it is properly cooked Siegfried touches the heart and burns his fingers. To ease the pain he puts his fingers in his mouth, and thus tastes the dragon's blood. The dragon's blood had magical powers and gave Siegfried the ability to understand the language

2

of the birds. Understanding the birds was a great advantage, for later they were able to warn the hero of the plans of his enemies.

However, the ancient Hebrews had a rather different attitude about man and his relationship to the animal world. According to the Bible, man was created in God's image. Man was also given dominion "over the fish of the sea, and over the fowl of the air, and over the cattle, and over all the earth, and over every creeping thing that creepeth upon the earth."

In this view man and animals were so completely different that it seemed impossible that animals could possibly possess the gifts of thought or speech. (Of course, the serpent in the Garden of Eden could and did tàlk. But this snake was not a "natural" animal.) The idea that there was an unbridgeable gap between man and animals was carried on by the early Christians.

But still, the ancient belief that animals could really talk persisted. So did the belief that man and the animals were able to communicate under special circumstances.

A large number of stories of talking animals grew up in Christian lands. The most famous is the story of the animals in Bethlehem that were given the gift of speech on the night of Christ's birth. Specially favored men could also communicate directly with the animals. St. Francis of Assisi was said to have regularly preached sermons to the birds.

Later in Europe a whole cycle of legends was developed around a hairy human-like creature called "the wild man." The wild man was a person who was supposed to have abandoned civilization, and gone off to live among the beasts of the forest. One of the things that the wild man could do was talk directly to the animals. This gave him great power in the forests.

Sometimes people were not quite sure what attitude they should adopt toward someone who had the reputation of talking to animals. Occasionally this sort of reputation resulted in serious trouble. In the seventeenth century there was a British magician named Banks who traveled around the world with his "talking" horse Morocco. To answer questions, Morocco tapped or stamped the ground with one of his front hoofs. By this method the horse could apparently add, subtract, and do other mathematical calculations as well as spell out words by a number code.

When Banks and Morocco appeared in the French city of Orleans, the performance so impressed the local citizens that some believed that supernatural forces were at work. Instead of assuming that Banks had gotten his ability to communicate with this animal from God, as St. Francis had, the people of Orleans decided he had been consorting with the devil—that he was a witch—and in the seventeenth century the charge of witchcraft was very serious. Many people had been hanged after being accused of witchcraft on flimsier evidence than the people of Orleans had against Banks.

The magician avoided being convicted of witchcraft

The "talking" horse Morocco and his master, the magician Banks

by a clever trick. He had Morocco walk up to a high dignitary of the Church and kneel down, as if in submission. The churchman and the common folk were de-

5

lighted by this display, and decided that no representative of the devil would come as close to a man of God as Morocco had. The charge of witchcraft was dropped. Banks and Morocco left Orleans gratefully, and in a hurry.

Most people did not get as upset about "talking" animals as the people of Orleans had. A whole variety of "talking" animals entertained people at fairs and circuses throughout Europe and America. One of the most famous was a creature called "The Learned Pig." For generations "The Learned Pig" performed regularly at fairs in England. (Actually there were a whole line of "Learned Pigs." When one pig got too old to perform another was substituted. None of the spectators knew the difference, since one pig looks pretty much like the next.)

"The Learned Pig," or at least *a* learned pig turned up in America. In 1798, William Frederick Pinchback announced that he had brought the famous pig over from England at great expense, in order to exhibit the creature to the people of Boston. The American "Learned Pig" was a great commercial success.

Pinchback was a professional magician and animal trainer. He even wrote a book called *The Expositor: or Many Mysteries Unravelled*. In the book he explained how he had trained his "Learned Pig." Pinchback also joked that if he had lived in Spain at the time he probably would have been brought before the Inquisition, on the charge of practicing witchcraft.

"Talking" animals were so commonly shown by magi-

GREAT ATTRACTION !

WONDER and ADMIRATION of the
WORLD !

THE LEARNED

NOVELTY &   AMUSEMENT!

PIG !

Mr JAMES L. HAZARD,

Respectfully informs the Ladies and Gentlemen of this place and vicinity, that the following performance of this

NOW, OR

NEVER !

EXTRAORDINARY PIG

cians and other performers that most people began to regard all the "talking" animals as tricks. A clever man might train an animal, even an animal as stubborn as a pig, to look as though it were answering questions. But in truth, the animal could not talk or understand. It could merely respond to the commands of its trainer.

Then, at the beginning of the twentieth century, there appeared in Germany a very remarkable "talking" animal. This animal's owner claimed that it had not been specially trained, but that it really could understand and answer very difficult questions.

2

The Tragedy of Clever Hans

In 1904, a group which included two distinguished scientists gathered in a courtyard in Berlin to witness a remarkable demonstration. In the center of the courtyard stood a beautiful horse named Hans. But everyone referred to this horse as *Der Kluge Hans*, Clever Hans.

Hans' owner was an elderly schoolteacher, Herr von Osten, and Hans had once pulled the old man's cart. But the horse impressed Herr von Osten as being much smarter than any other horse he had ever seen. The schoolmaster owned a large cart, and his home had a narrow curving driveway. Other horses would allow the cart to scrape the side of the driveway or bump against the gatepost, but not Hans. He always guided the cart through the driveway perfectly. How, the schoolteacher wondered, was Hans able to calculate the curve of the driveway so well.

Occasionally when in the stable Herr von Osten would talk to his unusually clever horse. We have all done the same sort of thing with a favorite pet, although we do not really expect the pet to answer. But Hans did sometimes answer, or at least Herr von Osten believed he did. The horse could not "talk" in the usual sense of the word —that is, he did not vocalize. But he could communicate by pawing the ground with his right front hoof. If Herr von Osten asked the horse to add two and two the animal would paw the ground four times—then stop.

Soon the mathematical questions became much more complicated. Herr von Osten found that his horse could add fractions. When he asked Hans to add two-fifths to one-half, Hans would paw the ground nine times, pause, and then ten times. The correct answer is nine-tenths.

This apparent genius among animals could do more than calculate, he could read. Hans was shown a numbered list of words. One of the words on the list was "oats," a word in which Hans must have had a genuine interest. When he was asked "Where is oats?" the horse would either point out the correct card with his nose, or indicate it by pawing the number in front of the word "oats."

Herr von Osten worked out a number alphabet, in which each letter or common combination of letters was a given number. With this Hans was able to spell words. Hans was shown a picture of a horse and asked what it was. He spelled out, with his number alphabet, *P f e r d*, the German word for horse.

Naturally, Herr von Osten told all his friends about this wonder horse, and was soon arranging private demonstrations of Hans' ability. The animal's fame spread. Even the Kaiser commented favorably on Clever Hans. A cartoonist of the day pictured Hans being formally examined by the Prussian Minister of Education himself. People claimed that the horse was as intelligent as an eleven-year-old boy—not an ordinary boy, but a Berlin boy. This was quite a compliment from the Berliners who were convinced that their children were the best educated in the world.

Hans was so famous that if Herr von Osten had wished to exhibit his horse at fairs and circuses he would have become a rich man. But the old schoolteacher was not interested in making money with the animal. What he wanted to do was to show the world that Hans was not only a genius among animals, but that he was able to communicate his thoughts to people. Herr von Osten was an honest man who believed completely in his horse's abilities and he invited scientists to come and test the animal.

Eventually an official scientific commission was appointed to examine Clever Hans. And so, in 1904, Professor Stumpf, a distinguished psychologist, and his associate Dr. Pfungst came to Berlin to see the horse. They devised a simple test. They had five numbered cards with five different words written on them. Card 1 had the word "stall"; card 2—"oats"; 3—"Hans"; 4—"Osten"; and 5—"key." Hans was instructed to tap the number 3 when the card with his name on it was shown to him.

Sometimes Herr von Osten was allowed to see the cards as they were shown to Hans, other times he was not. The results of this test were devastating for Hans and his master. Fourteen times when Herr von Osten knew which card was being shown, Hans tapped the correct number. Twelve times when he did not know which card was being shown, Hans did not tap correctly.

Other tests were conducted, and the results were always the same. Every time Herr von Osten knew the correct answer, Hans answered correctly. Every time he did not, the horse failed the test. Obviously, the old schoolteacher was signaling Hans in some way.

Herr von Osten was so clearly sincere in his belief that his horse could "talk" and had been so willing to cooperate with the tests that the scientists could not accuse him of deliberate fakery. They concluded that the old schoolteacher had been unconsciously signaling the horse when to start tapping and when to stop.

When he first began testing Hans it had been Herr von Osten's custom to reward the animal with a lump of sugar for every correct answer. Hans naturally wanted the reward and kept a close eye on his master during the test. The old man was very anxious for Hans to get the correct answer, so when the question was asked he would look directly at the horse's right front hoof, and lean forward slightly. Hans, who really was clever, interpreted this slight lean as a signal to start tapping. Sooner or later the desired number would be reached. When Hans had tapped the proper number of times, Herr von Osten would, again involuntarily, straighten up. So Hans would stop tapping and get his lump of sugar. The same sort of slight involuntary signs were used to get Hans to point to the correct word on a list.

The stooping and straightening up had been so slight that until Professor Stumpf and Dr. Pfungst began their investigations, no one had noticed it, although hundreds had seen Clever Hans in action. Soon the scientists themselves were able to start Hans tapping, by leaning forward slightly, and stop him by straightening up.

When the report of the scientific commission was published it destroyed Hans' reputation, and Herr von Osten's as well. Many people refused to believe that the old schoolmaster had not deliberately trained the horse in order to fool the public, although the report had made no such charge.

Herr von Osten never accepted the fact that he had been signaling Hans unconsciously. He denounced the commission's report. He died soon afterward—of a broken heart his friends claimed.

Hans passed into the care of one of Herr von Osten's friends, Karl Krall, a wealthy merchant who believed completely in the horse's ability. Herr Krall took Clever Hans to his estate in Elberfeld on the Rhine, but Hans would not answer any more questions. The poor animal was deeply depressed over his master's death and that is why he would not "talk," Herr Krall said. The merchant certainly did not believe the report of the scientific commission, and was not in the least discouraged by the sudden failure of Hans' power to answer questions.

Being a rich man, Herr Krall bought three magnificent Arab steeds named Muhamed, Zarif, and Mustapha. These he trained with the same methods that had been used by Herr von Osten. The horses learned to tap out answers with a front hoof. They, too, were rewarded with a lump of sugar for any correct answer.

Soon the three Arab horses seemed capable of outstripping even Clever Hans in their ability to answer difficult questions. Herr Krall taught his horses to use the left front hoof to indicate tens and the right front hoof to indicate units. Thus Muhamed, Zarif, and Mustapha could answer questions involving much larger numbers without tapping endlessly. Herr Krall also developed a simplified code of taps for the alphabet.

Muhamed astonished visitors to Herr Krall's estate by tapping out the correct answers to square root problems. When the famous dramatist Maurice Maeterlinck was brought to see the horses, all three tapped out his name as a greeting, even before they had been introduced. Maeterlinck was very flattered that the horses seemed to recognize him.

While Herr Krall was anxious to show off his horses to men like Maeterlinck, there was one sort of person who was not welcome at his estate, skeptical scientists like Professor Stumpf and Dr. Pfungst. He was taking no chance of ending up in disgrace like Herr von Osten.

In 1912, Herr Krall issued a large book called *Thinking Animals*. In the book he described, in great detail, his experiments with the three Arab horses. He claimed that he had taken every possible precaution against signaling the answers to the horses. But most scientists were unimpressed by Herr Krall's book. Dr. Stefan von Maday

14

issued a book almost as large as Herr Krall's in which he disputed practically every one of the merchant's conclusions. He said that Herr Krall had not really taken any effective precautions at all against signaling the horses, and that these horses were not answering any questions, but merely tapping in response to signals. Not only that, Dr. von Maday went on to analyze Herr Krall himself, and hinted that the merchant, unlike Herr von Osten, was not entirely unaware that he was signaling his horses.

The battle lines were clearly drawn. On the one side there stood the friends and followers of Herr von Osten and Herr Krall. They were convinced that the animal world contained some "geniuses." Such "genius" animals could learn to talk, do arithmetic, and read, but most importantly, they could communicate with human beings.

On the other side of the line stood most of the scientists. They believed, like Professor Stumpf, Dr. Pfungst, and Dr. von Maday, that these so-called "genius" animals were nothing of the sort, that they were just ordinary trained horses. The scientists said that these horses could not understand the questions that had been asked them, that all they did was to respond to certain signals given consciously or unconsciously by their trainers.

The scientists were, of course, correct but the controversy was very unfortunate. It set back any serious scientific attempts to communicate with animals for many years. Only recently have scientists again become interested in the problem of "talking to animals."

3

The Language of Animals

Today no scientist doubts that animals can "talk" if by talk we mean simply communicate with one another. Talking usually means passing information from one individual to another by vocalizing. That is the way that we do most of our communicating. But even though man is among the world's most vocal creatures, he still uses a great many signs other than vocalizations for communication. A shrug of the shoulders, a shake of the head, or a frown can often communicate more than words. Handshakes, pats on the back, and kisses are all, in their own way, a means of communication. They are signs that mean something to other individuals.

Therefore, a language can be more than words and rules of grammar. Any organized system of signs that is used for communicating information from one creature to another might be called a language. Certainly the most remarkable animal language yet discovered is the language of the bees.

Perhaps you have had this experience: You are at a picnic and you suddenly find a bee crawling around the rim of your soft drink cup. The bee has been attracted by the sugar in your drink. Bees can inflict a painful sting, so one bee is bad enough. But shortly after the first bee finally flies off, a half dozen more show up. And they are all making a "beeline" for your soft drink.

The bees did not just play "follow the leader" in finding their way to the picnic site. A bee that has discovered a rich source of food—in this case your soft drink—flies back to her hive and tells the other bees just exactly where the food is. This is no simple task. Try to imagine what sort of directions you would have to give to a friend in order to have him find a particular spot a mile or two away.

The means by which the bees communicate this very precise information—the language of the bees—was finally "translated" in 1943 by a patient German scientist named Karl von Frisch. Von Frisch had spent years watching honeybees living in a glass-walled hive. He marked some of these bees with spots of color so he could tell one from the other.

The scientist would put out dishes of sugar water, which the bees can use as food, just as they use the nectar from flowers or a sugary soft drink. When one of the bees would discover a dish of sugar water it would gather some of it up and fly directly back to the hive. As soon as it got to the hive the scout would distribute the food to the other bees. This alerted the other bees that a good food source had been located, and they would begin to crowd around the bee that had found the food. The

17

A honeybee

scout bee would then begin a series of very particular motions. Von Frisch labeled these motions "the dance of the bees." By means of this "dance" the bee communicated to other members of the hive the location of the food source she had discovered.

If the food source was close by, one hundred yards or less from the hive, the bee would go through a fairly simple series of motions, called by von Frisch "the round dance." This communicated to the other bees the simple message that there was food close by. A flying bee can easily scout an area within a radius of one hundred yards from its hive in a short time. The round dance might be translated as "food nearby, you can't miss it."

If the food was farther away the dance became more complicated because more information had to be communicated. In this dance the scout bee not only has to tell the others how far away the food is but also the direction in which it will be found. This is all communicated by what Dr. von Frisch called the "waggling dance."

The distance to the food is indicated by the speed at which the dance is performed. If the dancer's performance is complete in about a second and a half, the other bees know that the food is approximately 325 feet away. If the dance takes a full two seconds, then the food is a mile away, and so forth.

The basic pattern of the waggling dance is simple. The bee runs in a semicircle, then a straight line; makes another semicircle, and then another straight line parallel to the first. During the straight-line portion of the dance the bee waggles her body from side to side in a very distinctive way. It was this motion that inspired von Frisch's name for the performance.

Diagram of the "dance of the bees." The round dance is shown on the left, the waggling dance on the right.

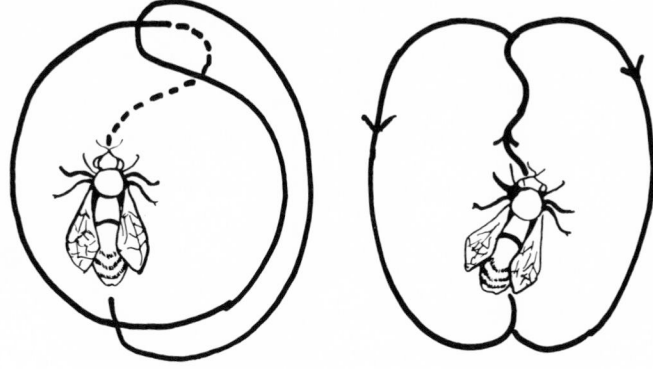

The part of the waggling dance in which the bee waggles in a straight line is the part which indicates the direction of the food. If the dance is performed outside the hive on a horizontal surface, the dancing bee shows her fellow workers where the food is by pointing herself toward it and making her waggling straight line in that direction.

In flight a bee navigates by the sun. The spectator bees determine the direction of the straight-line portion of the waggling dance in relation to the sun. If they stay on the same angle with the sun during their flight, they will be flying in the exact direction indicated by the dancing bee.

However, most of the dancing bee's performances do not take place outside the hive. A scout bee that has found food usually enters the hive before beginning her dancing performance. Thus the dance is most commonly performed in a place where the spectators cannot see the sun, and therefore cannot directly determine the angle at which they must fly.

These dances are also usually performed on the vertical comb of the hive. Therefore, when the dancer runs in a straight line she is running up or down the vertical surface, rather than in the actual direction of the food supply. Instead of actually pointing out the direction, the dancer's motions indicate it symbolically. Then it is up to the spectators to correctly interpret the symbols when they fly out in search of the food.

If the dancer on the vertical comb runs straight up

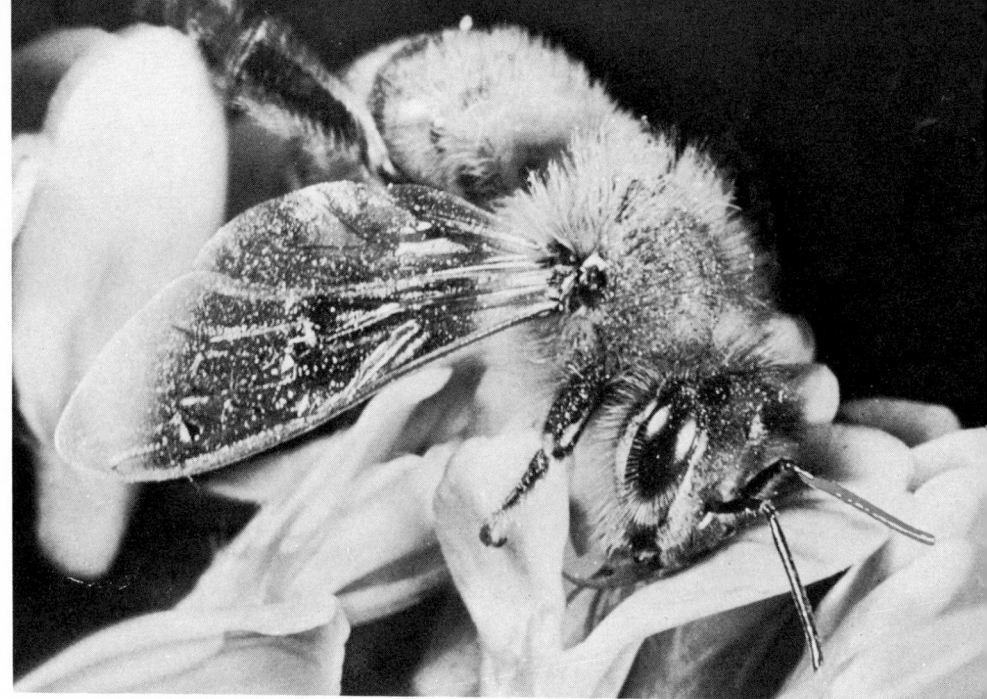

A honeybee that finds a rich supply of food flies back to the hive and communicates the location of the food to the other bees by means of a series of motions called "the dance of the bees."

during the waggling portion of the dance, this means that the food supply will be found by flying directly toward the sun after leaving the hive. If the dancer runs straight down, this means that the food will be found by flying directly away from the sun. If the dancer performs her waggling run while going up the comb, but the run points, let us say, ten degrees to the left of straight up, the spectator bees know that they are to fly ten degrees to the left of the sun, and so on.

The language of the bees is so exact that scientists who have learned it can watch a performance of the waggling dance and then go right to the spot that was indicated by the bee.

Other forms of bee dances are used to communicate other information. When a colony of bees is looking for a new place to build a hive, scouts are sent out to investigate possible homesites. These scouts return with "reports" about the desirability of the different spots they have seen. The "reports" are given in the form of a dance. The more vigorously the dancer performs, the better she believes her site to be. In this way the various sites are "debated" among the different scouts, while the rest of the colony watches. The scout that dances or "speaks" most vigorously in favor of the place she has investigated usually wins over the other bees. Finally, all fly off in the direction she has indicated.

As you can see, the bees with their dance language can communicate quite complicated information. Bees are probably better at giving and understanding directions than human beings are. But there are some very basic and important differences between the bee language and our own.

Although we were born with the potential ability to speak, we were not born knowing a language. We have had to learn the language we speak. If we grow up in a home where our parents speak English, we learn English. If we grew up in France, we would learn French; in Italy, Italian. The bees, however, do not *learn* their dance language—they seem to be born with the ability both to perform and understand the complicated dances. Their language is the result of what we call *instinct*.

For a long time many people believed that all animals acted almost completely by instinct—that is, that they were born with certain ways of behaving and could never change these patterns. Animals, according to this theory, never "thought about" anything they did. We know now that this view was not completely correct. Scientists today are very careful about using the word instinct, for they have found that even an animal like a bee, which seems to perform most of its acts by instinct, is capable of learning, of adjusting the patterns of its behavior to new conditions. For example, bees can change the "language" of their dance.

One of Dr. von Frisch's students, Martin Lindauer, took a hive of bees from the island of Ceylon to Germany. Ceylon is in the Southern Hemisphere, Germany in the Northern Hemisphere. When the bees were released they found that the sun was in a different place in the sky than they were accustomed to. Bees, you will recall, navigate by the sun.

If the bees were nothing more than machine-like prisoners of instinct, then they would not be able to change their habits and adjust to the new position of the sun. For several weeks these bees from Ceylon did seem thoroughly confused and unable to navigate properly by the northern sun. But after forty-three days, Lindauer found that they had adjusted completely, and they could navigate as well as any native German bee. The bees had learned—they were not merely prisoners of instinct.

While the language of the honeybee is very elaborate, most of the honeybee's close relatives, like the carpenter bee, do not have the ability to dance out instructions. Is the honeybee somehow more intelligent than the carpenter bee? No, not necessarily.

Over the centuries the language of the honeybee has evolved, but no similar development has taken place among carpenter bees because the honeybee needs the language and the carpenter bee does not. The honeybee is a social animal; it lives in a hive with thousands of other bees. No single honeybee can survive for long alone. When an individual bee finds a rich source of food, it can carry only a small amount back to the hive. But at the hive there are many other bees that could bring back the food if they were told where to go. The more precise the instructions, the better the chance of the other bees finding the food. In the long run, the better the ability of the honeybees to "speak" and "understand" one another, the better the chances for the survival and success of the hive and the species.

The carpenter bee, on the other hand, leads a largely solitary life. If it finds a rich source of food it takes what it can carry. But it has no hive to return to, and no one else to communicate the information to. For that reason there has never been any need for this kind of bee to develop a language.

Therefore, we can see that language alone is not a sign of intelligence. An animal language does not develop because an animal is smart; it develops because one animal needs to communicate with another. In general, social animals—animals that live in groups—have more highly developed languages than solitary animals.

4

The Language of Reaction

When a small baby gets hungry, he cries. His mother hears the crying and feeds him. The baby has communicated the message "I am hungry, feed me" very clearly to his mother. But the baby does not know that. When he is hungry he begins to feel uncomfortable, so he cries. The crying is an expression of an inner feeling rather than a conscious attempt to communicate. The crying is a *reaction*.

Most animal communication is the result of reaction, like the baby's crying. One of the most dramatic examples of this language of reaction occurs among rats. When two strange rats are put in the same cage they instantly communicate a great deal to one another. Their fur will bristle, their noses twitch, and their teeth will begin to chatter. They will approach one another cautiously, on tiptoe, and begin to circle. All of these signs mean one thing—"I am ready to fight."

Then, quite suddenly, one of the rats—usually the weaker of the two—will flop over on its side with its eyes half-closed. This is the rat's "surrender sign"; it means "You win, I give up." The winning rat could now easily kill his opponent by biting the fallen rat's throat with his own sharp teeth. But he doesn't. Seeing the "surrender sign," the winner turns and walks away stiffly. A little while later the loser himself gets up and goes his own way.

This entire "fight" takes a minute or less, but in that brief time a good deal of information has been communicated. However, as far as we know, neither rat "intended" to communicate anything. They just reacted to the feelings aroused within them by the situation. Yet the communication that resulted from this language of reaction prevented a bloody, and probably fatal, fight between the two rats.

The opossum's famous ability to "play possum" or play dead probably began with a surrender reaction like that of the rat. When the opossum is faced with a vastly stronger opponent—say, a dog—it will often flop over on its side with its eyes closed and its tongue lolling out. This looks like an extreme version of the rat's surrender reaction.

When in this state, the opossum can be pushed, pulled, and even picked up and shaken, but it will not move. The animal looks dead. This does not communicate the message "You win, I give up" to the dog; it communicates the message "I am dead." Most dogs will cheerfully kill a living opossum, but have little interest in a dead one. So the dog will shortly get bored and go its own way.

With the immediate danger gone, the opossum will recover or "come back to life."

The opossum did not "intend" to communicate the false message "I am dead" to the dog. When it became involved in a frightening and dangerous situation, the opossum's reaction was to appear as if it were dead. This reaction has doubtless saved the lives of many opossums.

Some people have argued that since most of the signs that animals use are reactions, and not conscious attempts at communication, animals do not really communicate. But this argument is not really fair.

A great deal of human communication is also based on the language of reaction. Something frightens us, and we scream. We are pleased, and we smile. If we become angry, we may shout or pound our fist on the table. All of these sounds, expressions, and gestures are very eloquent means of communication. Yet they are all reactions to immediate situations. Under stress of a strong emotion we will often say things we do not mean, or wish we had not said. This, too, is part of the language of reaction. But no one complains that this is not communication.

However, human beings can do some things that most animals cannot do. We do not have to be in an immediate situation to describe our reaction to it. We might tell someone how angry we had been, long after we have stopped being angry. Or we can describe how angry we might become if something happens in the future.

In his book *How Animals Communicate*, author Bil Gilbert puts the difference this way: "We might say that animal languages lack grammar. In most cases animals use and respond only to the 'present tense.'"

Animals are also unable to communicate abstract ideas. No dog can discuss the idea of justice or truth. On the other hand, most animals cannot lie either. They cannot feel one reaction and express another.

Perhaps the greatest difference between human and animal languages lies in the area of learning. Communication between animals takes place mostly by means of signs and symbols that are inherited. Human beings, on the other hand, seem to learn most of their ability to communicate. But even here there are no hard and fast lines. Even bees can learn a little bit, and other animals can learn a great deal. Therefore, not all animal communication is "instinctive" nor is all human communication thought out or "rational."

Animal behaviorist John Paul Scott describes the differences this way: "We may conclude that human language has evolved from capabilities which are present in a large variety of lower animals and that the chief differences lie not so much in possessing a different kind of basic ability as in the degree to which language has been developed and its importance in social organization."

If differences between human and animal communication are really just differences in degree, then communication between man and at least some members of the animal world should be possible. The task of breaking the language barrier between men and animals is, however, a big one. There are no animal "geniuses" that will quickly learn to count and spell as Herr Krall believed Clever Hans had done. But after years of patient and often frustrating work, some scientists have begun to "talk" to the animals.

5

A Little Bird Told Me

Of all the animals in the world, man has traditionally believed that he has the best chance of communicating with the birds. In all the legends about people who talked to animals, birds were always the favorite subjects for communication. One of the stories told about King Solomon, who was reputed to be extremely wise, contains the words: "All the birds had been summoned before Solomon."

The main reason that man has believed that he would be able to talk to the birds is easy enough to see, or rather to hear. Like men, birds are great noisemakers. Much of the communication among birds is done by vocalization.

Another strong reason for believing that we can communicate with birds is that birds are the only animals we know of that can successfully imitate human speech. Parrots have long been kept as pets because of their ability to "talk" or mimic human speech. The small parrot-like parakeet or budgerigar can also learn to imitate a few words, though it is not as good as its larger relative.

In recent years the Oriental myna bird has gained a

reputation of being even a better mimic than the parrot. However, the stories of myna birds or parrots having "vocabularies" of hundreds or thousands of words are exaggerations. Most of these birds can imitate only a few simple words or phrases.

Crows were also once kept as "talking" pets. According to some stories, only crows that had a split tongue would be able to "talk." This old wives' tale was nonsense, and cruel too, for some people would deliberately cut a crow's tongue, in the belief that they could then get it to talk. Any crow can learn to mimic a bit of human speech if it is properly trained while still young. Crows, however, are less adept at mimicry, and therefore harder to train than either parrots or myna birds.

Perhaps the most celebrated talking bird in the world is the crow's larger relative, the raven. This particular bird owes at least part of its talking fame to Edgar Allan Poe's poem, "The Raven." The raven in the poem only uttered a single word, "Nevermore," but some ravens have been taught to mimic fairly long phrases.

One of America's most common birds, the starling, is a close relative of the "talkative" myna bird. The starling can also be taught to mimic a few human words. In a strange way the starling owes its existence in America to this ability to mimic human speech.

Starlings are extremely common throughout Continental Europe and England, but until the 1890s there were no starlings in the United States. A few hundred years ago caged starlings were kept as pets in England and taught to say a few words. In William Shakespeare's play *Henry IV* there is a line: "Nay, I'll have a starling shall be taught to speak nothing but 'Mortimer!'"

This line came to the attention of Eugene Scheifflin, a wealthy New York City drug manufacturer. Scheifflin loved both birds and the plays of Shakespeare. It was his ambition to see all the birds mentioned by Shakespeare living wild in the United States.

In 1890, Scheifflin released a flock of starlings in New York City's Central Park. These birds first took up residence under the ornamental eves of the American Museum of Natural History, just across the street from the park. Within a few decades they had spread throughout the United States. Anyone who has ever heard a flock of starlings coming home to roost for the night knows that they are among the noisiest birds in the world.

None of the so-called "talking" birds—parrots, mynas, crows, starlings—really "talk," that is, communicate with human speech. Nor are human words that they utter outward reactions to inner feelings except in rare cases. The birds seem more like living tape recorders. They can "play back" words, but they do not know what the words mean.

A trained parrot may say "hello" when you enter the room. But it has no idea that it is giving you a greeting. It may also say "hello" when you leave, or simply repeat the word to an empty room. As far as we can tell, the parrot regards the word as just another noise. While birds have the ability to mimic human speech more closely

Myna birds are excellent mimics. Pictured is the white Bali myna. The black hill myna is a common pet.

than any other member of the animal kingdom, we have to conclude that this mimicry is not communication. Talking to a parrot is about as meaningful as talking to a tape recorder.

Although only a small number of birds can imitate human speech, a large number can imitate the songs and calls of other birds, or the noises made by other animals. Some starlings rarely use their own call, but spend most of their time giving calls that are typical of other species

33

of birds. Wild starlings have been known to give very convincing imitations of a cat.

Neither the mockingbird nor the catbird can mimic the human voice, but both can give excellent imitations of the songs of other birds. Even the common English sparrow can learn to sound a little bit like a canary if it is raised with canaries.

Most of an animal's abilities serve some sort of purpose. Zoologists say that these abilities have a "survival value," which means that in one way or another they have helped that species to survive. But no one knows what purpose or survival value the birds' talent for mimicry has. A number of theories have been advanced. Some believe that the mimicry is used to divert attention, or to drive off other birds. But there is no proof for these theories.

Perhaps the talent some birds have for mimicry does not serve any real purpose at all but is merely a by-product of the birds' development. Birds have to be able to mimic sounds, for many do not inherit their particular song patterns and must learn them by imitation.

A chickadee raised in a laboratory without ever hearing another chickadee will still utter its characteristic "chickadee" call. A Baltimore oriole or white-crowned sparrow raised in isolation will be able to sing, but the song of the isolated birds will be very different from that used by wild birds. Apparently these birds have to hear adult birds of their own kind singing before they can develop their normal song.

Pet owners have long known that canaries can be taught to sing many different songs.

Owners of pet birds have known for centuries that their birds could be trained to sing. Today you can go to a pet store and buy a record that is designed to teach a canary to sing. During the eighteenth and nineteenth centuries caged songbirds were taught to imitate various musical instruments.

In recent years some scientists have begun to investigate the songbird's ability to learn to sing. The problem is not simple. Every species seems to learn a different amount, and the learning takes place at a different time in each species. One thing is certain: most songbirds do learn to sing. They are the only other animals beside man that are known to learn a major portion of their language.

Since birds seem to learn their song, by mimicking members of their own species, perhaps birds like the parrot simply have an overdeveloped ability to mimic. It may be that parrots and other birds like them use mimicry because it provides them with a vocal exercise.

Bird mimicry may have no value for communication, but bird calls and songs very definitely do communicate information—at least of a general type. A few years ago a Pennsylvania State University professor observed that when a starling is frightened it lets out a loud shriek. Upon hearing that sound, other starlings fly away.

The professor made a record of starling distress shrieks. Then he got a sound truck and drove to a town that was infested with starlings. (Starlings are noisy and dirty birds; most people consider them pests and are glad to be rid of them.) The professor played his recorded starling distress call over the truck's loud-speaker system, with the volume turned up full. The town's starlings all took off, and they did not return. (What effect these loud shrieks had on the people who lived in the town is not recorded.)

Since that time a number of towns and cities have tried to drive away starlings with loud recordings of their distress calls. The method seems to work for a while, but starlings are extremely adaptable birds. They soon learned the difference between recorded distress calls and the real thing. Besides, the recording has to be played so frequently that the noise is much worse than the noise made by the real starlings.

Crows are also adaptable. Although they are best known for their rather raucous and raspy calls, they have a considerable vocal range and, as we noted, crows can be trained to imitate the human voice. Some observers believe that crows have as many as five different and distinct calls to express alarm. The emotions contained in these calls range from mild uneasiness to panic. When one crow lets out the "panic" call, the whole flock will take flight. Coincidentally, the alarm call that a crow gives when it sees a hawk sounds like a hoarse human voice calling "hawk, hawk."

Birds do not live in highly organized societies as do bees. However, many species of birds will gather in flocks which have more or less rigid social structures. Many of these birds seem to have a call—or a group of calls—which serves the purpose of keeping the flock together. The members of a group of grosbeaks foraging for food are always making chirping noises. These noises do not seem to produce any reaction in other members of the group; they just seem to mean "Here I am, here I am."

During the day starlings will forage over a wide area, but as evening begins to fall the starlings gather in large flocks for the homeward flight to their nighttime roosting place. First, a few starlings from outlying areas

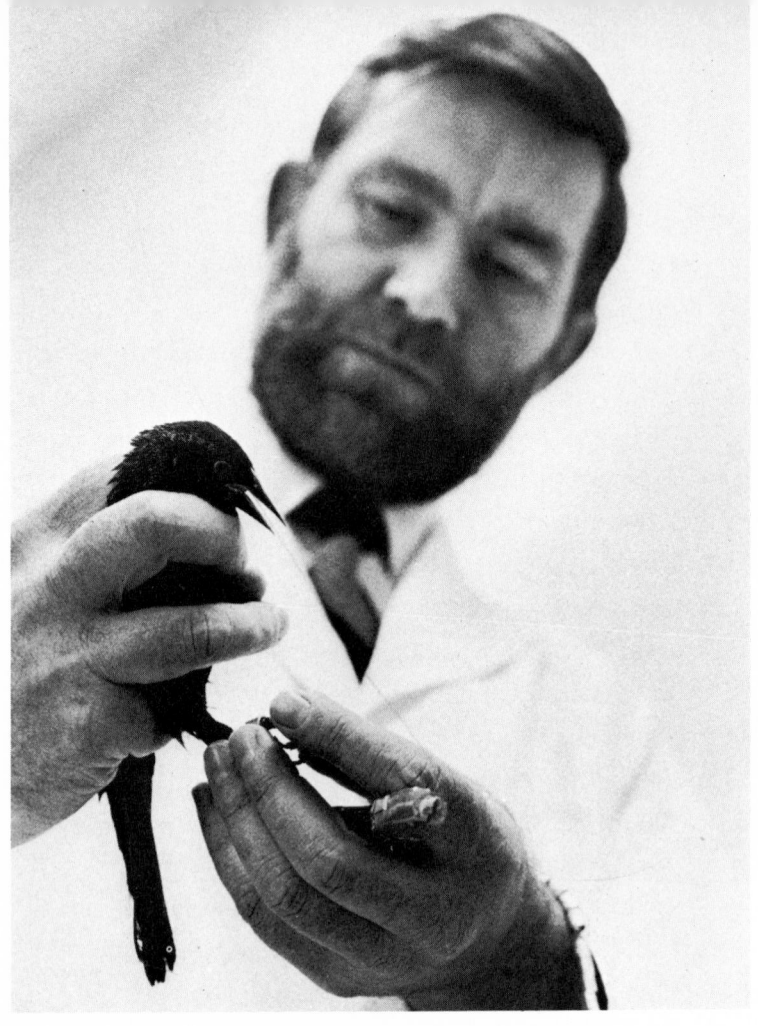

Dr. Peter Marler, who studies bird songs in the laboratory, puts a leg band on a red-winged blackbird.

gather. Their noises attract other starlings. The crowd grows and grows as it gets nearer the roosting place. Ultimately several thousand birds may come in to roost at once. The noise of the flock is unforgettable.

Migrating Canada geese continually make a loud honking sound. At night or in bad weather the honking of the geese might serve to keep the flock together.

Most birds, even those that live in flocks, tend to be more individualistic than cooperative, but they will sometimes help one another out, if it is not a great inconvenience. If a gull has found a small amount of food, it will devour the food in silence. However, if it discovers a large quantity of food—more than a single bird could possibly eat—then it gives a particular call. This call quickly attracts the other gulls in the vicinity.

The gull may have no "wish" to call the other members of its flock—it probably does not. The call may be little more than an uncontrollable expression of excitement and joy at seeing so much food. Other gulls would soon be able to recognize this cry and react to it by flying to the bird that had uttered it.

While some bird calls serve the purpose of keeping a

Dr. Marler and some of the subjects of his bird song experiments

group of birds together, a much larger variety of calls and songs is used to keep birds away from one another These are the territorial calls and songs. Many of the most beautiful bird songs, which man sentimentally likes to interpret as "love" songs, are really aggressive war cries. They could be roughly translated as "This is my land, keep out!" The territorial call may also serve as a mating call. A male loudly defending his territory attracts eligible females.

While they are among the most vocal of animals, birds do not communicate only by voice. They have a variety of gestures and displays which mean a great deal. This language of gesture and display is particularly striking during the mating season.

A male pigeon with his neck all puffed up, strutting persistently back and forth in front of an apparently disinterested female, is communicating something. So is the male peafowl (the peacock) that displays his gorgeous tailfeathers for a prospective mate.

Despite the many different means by which birds communicate, their messages seem simple. They express basic emotions—alarm at sensing danger, pleasure at finding food, desire to attract a mate. No bird seems capable of conveying to another the sort of complicated information contained in the dance of the bees.

This is not because birds are somehow less intelligent than bees. By any standard, the bird is a much more intelligent animal. Birds simply do not need to communicate as much. Some birds can get along on a bare minimum of communication. Hawks and other birds of prey, which lead rather solitary lives, seem to have relatively few meaningful calls or gestures. Gulls and geese, on the other hand, which live in large flocks, use a wide range of calls and gestures.

Many forest animals seem capable of understanding the bird's language—at least in a general way. If a flock of chickadees begins chirping their alarm call, other forest creatures will fall silent, as if expecting danger. Yet the animals will show no particular reaction to any of the chickadees' other calls.

While scientists have been able to understand the language of the bees, the communication can only be one-way. It is physically impossible for a man to say anything in the dance language of the bees. A man weaving about in a human imitation of the waggling dance would mean nothing to the bees. In fact, it is rather ridiculous even to imagine such an attempt. But we are quite capable of communicating with the birds in their own language. The hunter who uses a duck call is, in a sense, communicating with the ducks, although his message is a false and deadly one.

Perhaps the man who has done more "talking" to birds than anyone else is the great Austrian naturalist Konrad Lorenz. Lorenz has devoted his life to the study of animals. He is considered the father of the science of ethology, the study of the behavior of animals in their natural surroundings. During his long career, Lorenz has worked with many different kinds of animals, par-

41

ticularly with birds. He and his associates "talk" quite regularly with the birds they study.

Once Lorenz and a friend, Dr. Alfred Seitz, went to a lake with a large group of graylag geese and mallard ducks. Lorenz fell asleep while Dr. Seitz attempted to take motion pictures of the graylag geese. But the mallards kept swimming into the picture.

"I was falling asleep," Lorenz wrote, "then suddenly, through the drowsy dimness of my senses, I heard Alfred say, in an irritated tone: 'Rangangangangang rangangangangang—Oh, sorry, I mean—quaha, gegegegegeg, quah, gegegegegeg.' I woke laughing; he had wanted to call away the mallards and had, by mistake, addressed them in graylag language."

In his years of working with birds, Lorenz encountered many parrots, crows, and other "talking" birds. Most of them, he noted, are very hard to train, and gave their human imitations at random. Occasionally, however, he found some of these birds which seemed to be able to make a connection between the human words they spoke and some outside occurrence.

One example concerned a parrot named Pappagallo (the Italian word for parrot) which belonged to the scientist's brother. The bird was allowed to fly freely outside the house. Pappagallo was very brave, but he had a mortal fear of the chimney sweep. Lorenz guessed that the black-garbed chimney sweep somehow reminded the parrot of a hawk or some other bird of prey. One day Lorenz observed Pappagallo, who had been sitting on

Members of the parrot family are famous for their ability to mimic human speech.

top of the house, suddenly take off shrieking, "The chimney sweep is coming, the chimney sweep is coming." From his lofty perch, the bird had seen the man coming down the road. Pappagallo had never been deliberately taught that phrase. Apparently he had learned the words from hearing the cook call them out when the chimney sweep appeared.

Since it is very difficult to teach a parrot a simple

phrase or even a single word, Pappagallo's feat was really remarkable. But Lorenz suspects that learning a phrase comes more quickly to birds when they are in a state of great emotional excitement; they somehow connect the phrase with the excitement.

However, Lorenz is extremely cautious about drawing too many conclusions from such incidents. He writes: "In such cases, the sentimental animal lover, crediting the creature with human intelligence, will take an oath on it that the bird understands what he says. This, of course, is quite incorrect. Not even the cleverest 'talking' birds, which, as we have seen, are certainly capable of connecting their sound expressions with particular occurrences, learn to make practical use of their powers, to achieve purposefully even the simplest object."

He describes how a scientist who had the greatest success in training birds was unable to teach a very clever parrot to say "food" when he was hungry and "water" when he was thirsty. Nor has anyone else ever been able to teach a parrot to "talk" in such a way. "The bird is able to connect his sound utterances with certain occurrences; we should expect him, first of all, to connect them with a purpose, but this surprisingly, he is unable to do."

Lorenz concludes that when your dog nuzzles you, whines, runs to the door, and scratches, "The dog wants to make you open the door. He is doing something very purposeful. This is far closer to human speech than anything a bird is capable of doing, no matter how human the bird may be able to sound."

6

Between Man and Dog

There is no better example of successful communication between different species of animals than between man and dog. When you think about it, this is not surprising. Both men and dogs are sociable creatures. Both are basically hunters. They have lived and worked together for a very long time. And, most important, both are thoroughly domesticated. By that we mean that they are far removed from life in the wild, and well adapted to the new challenges of civilization. In civilization the communication between species is much more important than it is in the wild.

Just when the long partnership between man and dog began we cannot say with any certainty. But it is not hard to imagine how it began. The wild ancestors of today's domestic dogs began hanging around the camps of prehistoric hunters. The dogs were attracted by the smell of cooking or rotting meat. Hungry dogs would steal bones and bits of meat when the hunters were not looking.

These wild dogs were probably first regarded as a

45

nuisance by the hunters. Yet the dogs were not big enough or fierce enough to be a real danger, so they were tolerated. Eventually the hunters might have come to appreciate the dogs' habit of cleaning up the camp-site. If the hunting band's supply of meat was properly guarded, the hunters could make sure that the dogs would only get the bones or other portions of the kill that were of no use to the humans. Later, perhaps hundreds or thousands of years later, the hunters began deliberately feeding these dogs to make sure that they would stay close to the camp. The dogs, instead of circling warily about the outskirts, would be given free run of the camp.

When did this process of taming, or domesticating, dogs begin? Some scientists believe that man started deliberately feeding dogs 50,000 or more years ago. But prehistoric man changed his ways at a painfully slow pace. It was another 30,000 years before the dog became an important part of man's life; that is, that the dog was changed from a wild animal that lived near man, to a fully domesticated animal that lived with man and served him. All of these dates are simply educated guesses. The earliest solid evidence we have of domesticated dogs comes from about 10,000 years ago, though it is safe to assume that domestication started long before that.

When the prehistoric hunters went out to stalk their prey, a pack of wild dogs trotting expectantly behind would have proved surprisingly useful. Dogs have a much keener sense of smell and hearing than men have.

The dogs would have become aware of the presence of other animals well before the hunters. The barking or baying of the excited dogs would have alerted the hunters that game was nearby. This was an early and very simple form of communication between man and dog. Possibly the barking helped to drive the deer or wild pig from its hiding place so that the hunters could attack it. The reward for the dogs would have been a chance to steal a piece of meat from an animal that they themselves were not large enough, or strong enough, to kill.

Obviously, this communication was unplanned at first. The men had not brought the dogs along on their hunt on purpose; at first, the hunters must have tried to drive away these persistent followers. For their part, the dogs could not help barking. They didn't "intend" to communicate anything to the hunters; it just happened. But after a while—a very long while—the hunters would have realized the usefulness of their noisy followers.

Another form of simple and unintentional communication would have been useful to the early hunters. Dogs have a strong territorial feeling. They resent intruders into the area they consider their home. These wild dogs would have come to regard the hunters' camp as a part of their territory. At night the wild dogs prowling just beyond the light of the campfire would bark or growl at any intruder. These noises would warn the hunters that something potentially dangerous, perhaps a saber-toothed cat or the members of a hostile band of hunters, was approaching in the dark.

47

When men began to domesticate other animals such as sheep and cattle, another talent of the dog would have come in handy. Dogs are natural herders. For a wild dog, or a pack of wild dogs, to attack directly a large herd of deer or wild cattle would be suicidal. The dogs would soon be cut to ribbons by a multitude of horns and hoofs. So the wild dogs would begin to divide the herd into smaller units, by driving the hunted animals first one way and then another. Finally, they would be able to isolate a single individual that they were able to kill. Wild wolves still hunt reindeer and caribou in this manner. Keeping the animals in a man's flock or herd from straying is not so very different from what dogs did naturally.

Yet the close relationship between man and dog is based on something more than mutual advantage. Men like to have dogs around, even when they serve no purpose at all. Dogs seem to like to be around men, even if they may be treated badly. This bond between the species is something we do not really understand yet.

Today there are a fantastic number of different kinds or breeds of dogs. They range from huge dogs, like the St. Bernard and great Dane, to tiny almost mouselike toy dogs, like the Chihuahua. Dogs can have long, pointed snouts, like the collie, or pushed-in faces, like the bulldog. There is no single animal species in the world that has as many variations as the domestic dog. The breeds vary in temperament and personality as much as in appearance.

Can all of these different kinds of dogs have descended from the same wild ancestor? Some authorities—like

North American wolf. Scientists believe that all domestic dogs are descended from wolves or jackals.

Konrad Lorenz, for example—believe that most of today's domestic dogs are descended from the jackal, a wild dog that still roams the desert regions of the Middle East and North Africa. The jackal is more of a scavenger than a hunter; therefore, it would have been quickly attracted to hunters' camps. It is also smaller and easier to tame than the larger and more ferocious wolf. Lorenz also believes that some of today's dogs—Alaskan sled dogs, chows, and a few other breeds—are descended from wolves. Dogs that are descended from wolves, Lorenz says, behave quite differently than those descended from jackals.

Other authorities disagree. From studying the bones of

ancient dogs, they conclude that all of today's domestic dogs are descended from some sort of small wolf. In this view, the tremendous differences in both appearance and personality have all developed since the dogs were domesticated.

Wolves are social animals that live and hunt in packs. They must have an effective system of communication within their own pack. Without it they would not be able to live together or hunt cooperatively.

Wolves have a bad reputation for being vicious, but this reputation is not deserved. The wolf pack is a well-ordered world, and wolves rarely fight seriously with one another. The status system within the pack—that is, knowing who gives way to whom—is rigidly maintained by a complicated "language." This language involves not only vocalizations, growls, barks, and whines, but various sorts of postures, facial expressions, and odors. Vocalizations are perhaps the least important part of the wolf's language.

The language of the wild wolf pack has been greatly modified in the dog after centuries of domestication. Complicated communication between members of a pack is not really necessary, because most domestic dogs do not live in packs. (Two groups of dogs that do live in packs, fox hounds and sled dogs, behave very differently from one another. All members of a hound pack look to the humans as their leaders. A pack of sled dogs, however, has a definite canine leader; only this leader makes any attempt to "communicate" with humans.)

50

A large part of the wolf's language is impossible for many domestic dogs. The position of a wolf's tail communicates a lot, but some breeds of domestic dog have their tails cut off. Others, like the chow, have tails that curl backward and can be moved very little. Such a dog cannot raise his tail in triumph as a wolf may do, or put his tail between his legs in humiliation and shame.

Facial expression among wolves is one of the principal means of communication. But who can know the facial expression of an old English sheep dog whose face is permanently covered with hair? When a wolf's ears are straight up he is usually feeling friendly, but when his ears are laid back flat, then he is frightened or angry. But a beagle, and many other breeds of dog, have long floppy ears and cannot either pick them up or lay them back to express friendship or anger.

Some modern breeds of dog like the old English sheep dog cannot communicate by their facial expressions or by the position of their tail.

Domestication has broken up the pack status known to wild dogs and has confused or destroyed many of the old means of communication between dogs. For this reason, serious fights occasionally do take place among domestic dogs. One dog often does not "understand" what another is "saying." The only alternative is to fight.

There is a common belief that the domestic dog is somehow less intelligent than the wolf, and that all animals "get soft" and degenerate mentally after centuries of domestication. Like most generalizations, this one contains a bit of truth and a lot of unproven and unprovable prejudice. The intelligence of wolves and dogs has never really been compared scientifically. Wolves would not be very cooperative in taking intelligence tests. An even more basic problem is that few scientists will agree on a definition of the word intelligence.

The wolf living a wild and free life in the forest survives because it has a whole range of adaptations to that sort of life. Aside from its intelligence, which cannot be accurately measured, the wolf has big teeth, strong jaws, and a powerful body. A pet dachshund could not adapt to the wolf's forest life, but the reason it could not is that the dachshund is not strong enough; lack of intelligence has nothing to do with it. The wolf would be no more capable of adapting to the dachshund's life in a city apartment.

The domestic dog does not have to communicate with other dogs, as the members of a wolf pack have to communicate with other wolves. The domestic dog must communicate primarily with the human beings whose life he shares. As a result, the domestic dog is often far better at communicating with people than it is at communicating with other dogs.

Some dogs will grab at their leash or scratch at the door when they want to be taken out. Some will carry their food bowl to their master, or stare fixedly at the cupboard in which their food is kept when they are hungry. This communication is certainly different and more effective than anything that wolves do in the wild. Domestic dogs usually learn to communicate such desires without being taught.

The dog that jumps about and barks wildly when he sees or otherwise senses that his master is returning is doing something that he did not inherit from his wild ancestors. That is something he learned all by himself. Says Konrad Lorenz: "No fixed instinct impels a dog to express affection by laying his head on his master's knee, and it is for this reason that such an action is more nearly related to our human language than anything that 'wild animals' say to one another."

Most domestic dogs are more vocal than their wild ancestors. A dog owner can understand a surprising amount about what his dog feels by listening carefully and learning to recognize the different vocal signs. An angry bark sounds quite different from a frightened bark. Posture and facial expression, even though they are less meaningful for domestic dogs than for wolves, can still convey a great deal.

For all its wrinkles, the English bulldog has an expressive face.

While a man can become adept at reading the expression on his dog's face, the dog may be even better at reading the expression on his master's face. Our prehuman ancestors must have carried on a good deal of communication by grimaces and face-making. Since we have developed a spoken language, we rely less on this sort of communication, although facial expression is still important. The wild dog also communicated a good deal by facial expression; but dogs do not have a spoken language. While some domestic dogs have lost the ability to express a great deal with their face, they have not lost the ability to observe and interpret expressions in others.

Our dogs watch us very closely. We are often surprised

by how much they seem to know about what we are feeling. If you are sad or depressed, it shows in your face, your posture, and the tone of your voice. A dog can observe this mood, and many will react to it by displaying various signs of sympathy. A crisis in the house will upset the family dog because the dog can see that all the humans around him are upset.

Some people have been a little too impressed by their dog's ability to understand them. They begin to believe that the dog has some sort of uncanny ability to read their mind. This, of course, is not true. Most people show their feelings very clearly with their face or tone of voice. Then they wonder how the dog knows what they are feeling. The dog is just a good observer. No one has ever claimed that "mind reading" is involved when two strange dogs quickly determine which is to be boss by mutual expressions, sounds, and posture. Yet just the same sort of observation is involved.

You may have heard that dogs know when someone is afraid of them because they can "smell fear." Dogs do have an excellent sense of smell, but they depend more on their eyes and ears to know who is afraid. When we are very frightened some chemical changes take place in our bodies. These may result in a subtle difference in body odor. But this difference is probably too slight to be detected by the average dog. If a dog frightens us, we show it, no matter how hard we try to cover up the fear. The dog can see that we are afraid.

We know a dog can learn a great deal from our tone

55

of voice. We use one tone when we call his name for dinner, and another when we discover that he has chewed up a slipper. One call will bring him running, the other will send him crawling under the couch. Can a dog understand our words, rather than just our tone of voice? Most people believe not.

In a book on animal intelligence the writer, Vance Packard, stated: "Select some command which he [your dog] normally obeys and which he seems to understand, such as 'Rover, roll over!' But change your tone. For example, say it softly and casually. If the psychologists are right, Rover will just stare at you. Or, better still, stick to your usual tone and gestures but use nonsense words such as 'Blowbar, mole lobber!' Then, presumably, Rover will roll over, unless he happens to be an extraordinarily alert dog."

This opinion is sharply disputed by Konrad Lorenz and others. Lorenz tells of an animal psychologist named Sarris who named his three dogs Harris, Aris, and Paris. "On command from their master, 'Harris (Aris, Paris), go to your basket' the dog addressed and that one only would get up unfailingly and walk sadly, but obediently, to his bed." Lorenz added that the command would be obeyed just as well if Sarris was in one room and the dogs in another, so he could not hint which dog was being ordered to bed by a glance or some other involuntary signal.

We should not be surprised that dogs can tell the difference between words and begin to associate these words with certain people, objects, or events. Dogs have a sense of hearing that is much keener than ours. People who want to downgrade a dog's intelligence often say that dogs are "trained" to recognize their own names, and therefore somehow do not really understand them. But how do human beings learn a language except by training? Of course, the dog can understand only a tiny number of words, compared with the words that can be understood by even a small child. But dogs can also recognize and understand sounds that human beings cannot even hear.

A dog can hear his master's footsteps long before human ears can pick them up. The dog can tell those particular footsteps from any others. He can distinguish the sound made by the family car from the sound made by any other car. People often attribute the dog's ability to know that someone familiar is coming to the fact that he can "smell them." But the dog depends more on his hearing than on his sense of smell for this ability.

However, as we have noted, the dog does have an excellent sense of smell. Wild dogs communicate a great deal by odor. The male among some species of wild dogs will mark out the territory he considers to be his by lifting his leg and spraying a few drops of urine on "boundary markers"—trees or rocks. A strange dog will then quickly be able to tell that he is entering someone else's territory.

The importance of the sense of smell seems diminished in many domestic dogs. Yet the bloodhound, and a few other breeds of dog, have a much more highly developed sense of smell than any wolf.

Dogs still sniff one another very thoroughly when they meet for the first time, and when you meet a dog he cautiously sniffs your shoes, legs, and hands before he will relax and allow himself to be patted comfortably.

The wolfish practice of marking out territory by scent has been continued by the domestic dog. Many domestic dogs will mark any convenient tree or post with a few drops of urine. On some city streets the same spot may be marked regularly by twenty or thirty different dogs. These "community scent boards," as some authorities call them, are carefully sniffed and marked by every passing dog. They seem to serve the purpose of letting the passers-by know who has been there before them.

Anyone who has ever owned a dog knows that man and dog can and do communicate. Some people become very attached to their dogs, and begin to regard them as highly, or more highly, than their human companions. Therefore, it isn't surprising that some people should have claimed that they could talk to their dogs as well or better than they could talk to people.

"Talking" dogs have long been shown at circuses and carnivals, although these dogs were viewed only as performers that had learned clever tricks. No one thought they could really "talk." Other "talking" dogs, like Miss Henny Kinderman's dog Lola, were of quite a different order. Miss Kinderman was a German lady who had been much influenced by the stories of Clever Hans and Herr

Krall's horses of Elberfeld. Miss Kinderman taught her dog an alphabet of taps like that used by the "talking" horses. However, rather than rapping on the ground, Lola would tap her mistress's palm.

The horses tapped openly and loudly. Anyone watching them could count the number of raps and determine for himself whether the animal had tapped the correct answer. Such openness was impossible with Lola. Observers could never be quite sure how many taps the dog had made on her owner's palm. It was up to Miss Kinderman to tell others whether or not her dog had tapped out the correct answer. Lola's answers were always correct, according to Miss Kinderman.

If this were not suspicious enough, Lola did not confine herself to answering questions. She soon began to make predictions about the weather. When asked how she knew so much, the dog is supposed to have replied that all dogs had taken an oath not to reveal their secrets. Silly as this sounds, a lot of people took Lola very seriously. Farmers would postpone mowing hay if Lola predicted rain.

At best, this rapping code for talking animals is cumbersome, and it takes a very long time for a dog or horse to rap out even a simple message. Some owners of "talking" dogs have tried to shorten the process. Stage performers trained dogs that would spell out words by picking up cards with letters on them. Soon people who really believed that they owned "talking" dogs had adopted the same technique.

A few trainers attempted to teach their dogs to vocalize intelligible human words. Herr Krall is said to have tried to teach this sort of vocalization to one of his horses, but here he met complete failure. The horse was capable of making nothing but horse noises. In frustration, he shouted at the horse, "Why don't you say 'Papa'?" The disgraced horse is said to have replied in its rapping alphabet, "'Cause I haven't got a good voice."

A dog is capable of making more different sounds than a horse, and so the dogs were a bit more successful at vocalizing. But the success was small. The best of the vocalizing dogs, a Doberman owned by Mrs. Alma Schmidt of Germany, was able to growl out only seven words. And these words were so indistinct that not everyone who heard them was sure that they were words at all. Only after Mrs. Schmidt "interpreted" the dog's noises did anyone know what the dog had been "saying."

A new technique has been added to this attempt to communicate with dogs by a woman in California named Elisabeth Mann Borgese. She had a specially designed electric typewriter constructed for her English setter, Arli. The machine has only twenty-one keys, and each of these keys is very large, for Arli must push them with his nose. Mrs. Borgese believes that in two years of training the dog learned seventeen letters and could compose some sixty words.

It does not seem that Arli's communication is really on a much higher level than that of Clever Hans. When Mrs. Borgese dictates a simple word, like cat or car, the dog can type it out, but this is accomplished only after numerous mistakes and false starts. It is doubtful that the dog has any more knowledge of the "meaning" of the words he is typing than the horses of Elberfeld had of the "meaning" of the square root problems they were supposedly answering.

When Mrs. Borgese would not dictate to Arli and the dog was given free reign over the typewriter, he usually typed only nonsense words. Some of Arli's meanderings over the keyboard were later broken up and arranged in lines so that they would look like short poems. One literary critic seriously compared these poems with some modern poetry. Arli's "poems" were composed mostly of nonsense words.

Despite the doubtful and disappointing results of tests of "talking" dogs and other canine "geniuses," we can see that man and dog have achieved a fairly high order of communication with one another. The feeling that many dog owners have that their pet understands much more than it can express is probably accurate.

As much as we may love our dogs, scientists feel that dogs are not the most intelligent creatures in the animal world. The great apes—chimpanzees, gorillas, and orangutans—are much more closely related to man. Scientific tests indicate that apes are more intelligent than dogs. For that reason, communication between man and the great apes should be easier and more successful.

A confirmed dog-lover like Konrad Lorenz disagrees. Lorenz believes that the dog will always be better at understanding "human talk" than an ape. The dog, he points out, is thoroughly domesticated and therefore freed of many of its instinctive behavior patterns. This leaves the dog open to develop new behavior patterns, such as the development of language. In addition, the dog seems to crave and need human companionship and approval. For this reason, a dog would be more interested in what people said than an ape would, and the dog would concentrate more of its energies on attempting to understand the humans around it.

7

Apes in the Wild

The Roman naturalist Pliny, who lived during the first century A.D., wrote about a strange race of men from the "Mysterious East." He called these men the Silvestres. They were said to be a wild people whose bodies were covered with long hair. They had yellow eyes and large pointed teeth. To top off this picture of horror, the Silvestres communicated only by means of loud shrieks. The Silvestres were not products of Pliny's imagination. He had heard a garbled description of some sort of ape.

Many ancient stories about hairy wild men began just as the story of the Silvestres must have begun, when some traveler unexpectedly encountered an ape. To a person who has never seen an ape before, the sight of one could be quite unnerving. These ancient travelers must have believed that nothing could look as human as an ape and not really be human. The name orangutan means "wild man" in the Malay language spoken by the people of Borneo and Sumatra.

The first apes that scientists had a chance to study closely were captive specimens. No one doubted that

In the Malay language, orangutan means "wild man."

apes were very clever animals. They quickly surpassed all other creatures (except man, of course) in certain sorts of intelligence tests devised by scientists. But where the apes fell far short of man's abilities was in the area of language. Like Pliny's Silvestres, apes seemed to communicate by shrieking.

The problem is that simply observing apes, or any other animals, in captivity does not give an accurate picture of the animal's intelligence and ability to communicate. A single chimpanzee in a cage doesn't "say" very much because it doesn't have any one to "talk" to. Even a captive colony of apes is living under conditions which are too artificial and too restricted to give a good picture of the sort of communication that can take place among these animals.

All the great apes—the orangutan, the gorilla, and the chimpanzee—live in areas that are far from the centers of civilization. These jungle regions are wild and it is difficult for man to live in them for any length of time. Besides, in the wild the great apes are very shy and hard to get close to. And if one does get close to them, there is always an element of danger, for apes are strong and unpredictable.

The orangutan is extremely rare and may be headed for extinction in the wild. It has never been studied thoroughly in its natural habitat, but during the last few years some dedicated and adventurous scientists have undertaken tremendous hardships in order to observe the lives of the two other great apes, the gorilla and the chimpanzee, in the jungle. As a result of these studies, we have to revise drastically our attitude toward communication among the great apes.

The gorilla is the largest of the great apes. Because of its huge size (an adult male can easily weigh 400 pounds) and strength, the gorilla has been greatly feared and thoroughly misunderstood. The gorilla was once a standard character in horror movies. It was depicted as a fierce creature that habitually tore men limb from limb and carried off beautiful girls. The most famous of all of these Hollywood horror gorillas was the gigantic King Kong. Even today, when you mention the word gorilla, a lot of people think first of King Kong. Circuses added to the

65

gorilla's undeserved reputation for ferocity by billing their captive gorillas as being the fiercest and most dangerous creatures alive.

But gorilla ferociousness was a myth, and the zookeepers and animal trainers knew it. Certainly, the gorilla was powerful enough to be very dangerous if angered, but a man was more likely to be squeezed to death in an affectionate hug, than to be torn limb from limb by a raging gorilla.

How do these giants of the ape world live in the jungle? Dr. George Schaller, a young American zoologist, went into the rain forests of the Congo in Africa in order to observe gorillas close up. He spent months virtually living among the wild gorillas. He was usually alone and unarmed, yet the gorillas never hurt him. Dr. Schaller concluded that even in the jungle these animals were very amiable.

Another myth that was shattered by Dr. Schaller's study was that the gorilla is a noisy animal, always roaring and beating its chest. On the contrary, he found them to be fairly silent creatures. In his months of observing gorillas, Dr. Schaller noted twenty-one more or less distinct vocalizations. Many of these were not loud, and most were used infrequently. Gorillas scream or roar only when badly frightened, furiously angry, or otherwise in a state of high excitement.

Gorillas are famous for beating their chests and roaring, however. Some people believed that the chest-beating display was like a war cry, and prelude to attack.

Photograph by Alan Root © National Geographic Society

Mountain gorilla beating its chest

Others thought that chest-beating was a bluff to scare off enemies. Dr. Schaller decided that it is neither. He saw that gorillas would beat their chests when they felt threatened by an enemy, but they would do the same thing when they were merely excited. The real reason for the chest-beating seemed to be tension or excitement.

As tension builds up in a gorilla he has to release it. He does so by engaging in a chest-beating display. Sometimes when we are very angry we will break something, or jump up and down and shout. These actions release tension. The gorilla does the same sort of thing when he beats his chest.

During this display the gorilla does a great deal more than just thump his chest; he hoots loudly, shuffles about, slaps the ground, breaks off branches, throws stones and earth, and even shoves food into his mouth.

The chest-beating gorilla is not trying to communicate anything or scare anyone. He is merely reacting to his own inner feelings. The display is so loud and frightening that it probably does scare potential enemies, although the gorilla did not intend anything of the sort. The chest-beating display of the gorilla is a very dramatic example of the language of reaction.

While gorillas do not make many different sounds, the "meaning" attached to these basic sounds can vary a good deal. Much depends on the tone or loudness of the sound, or the circumstances under which it is made. Dr. Schaller tells of one female gorilla that would scream loudly in fear every time she saw him. The other gorillas had long since gotten used to the scientist's presence, and simply took him for granted. Writes Dr. Schaller: "The others ignored her warning, even when she was out of sight, indicating that they recognized her voice. Apparently she had cried 'Wolf!' too often."

Gestures, postures, and expressions—not vocalizations—

The lowland gorilla

are the most important means of communication among gorillas, Dr. Schaller believes. The noises that a gorilla makes are just a secondary part of its language. Vocalizations seem to serve the purpose of catching the attention of the other gorillas. After attention is fixed on the "speaker," more specific information is communicated by means of some gesture, posture, or expression.

In order to communicate the idea that the tribe should move on from the place where they were resting, the dominant male, who leads the tribe, does not have to make a sound. He simply gets up and starts walking with a particular determined and stiff-legged walk. The rest of the tribe almost always follows him. On the other hand, if the dominant male simply wants to move to a different spot within the rest area, he walks at a more leisurely pace, and the others take no particular notice of him.

Once, Dr. Schaller felt that he was really communicating with the gorillas in their own language. When two friendly gorillas meet they sometimes stop and shake their heads back and forth. Dr. Schaller translated this gesture as meaning "Peace, I intend no harm." When Dr. Schaller unexpectedly encountered a gorilla he would attempt to pacify the animal by shaking his own head back and forth. The gesture seemed to work.

In the end, however, the scientist was distinctly unimpressed by the ability of these peaceable primates to communicate with one another:

"As I watched the gorillas over the weeks and months, a subtle change occurred in my thinking about the apes. At first I was highly impressed with their human ways, but there was something basic lacking, something that their brown eyes, no matter how expressive, could not convey, namely, a means of communication with each other about the past and the future and about things that were not immediately apparent. In other words, the gorillas lacked a language in the true sense of the word."

Dr. Schaller finally concluded that the signaling system used by the gorillas was really no more complex than that used by dogs and some other animals.

Recently, another gorilla watcher has gone into the field. She is Miss Dian Fossey of California. Although she is not a trained zoologist, Miss Fossey has had tremendous success in getting close to the big apes. She believes that one of the reasons they have accepted her is that she imitates their actions and gestures.

Miss Fossey confirms that the gorilla is more bluff than danger. Once, she was charged by five roaring male gorillas. She stopped them, when one was only three feet away, by simply spreading her arms and shouting, "Whoa!"

The gorilla's relative, the chimpanzee, may be better at communication. Most scientists agree that the chimpanzee is more intelligent than the gorilla. Chimpanzees are certainly a lot noisier and seem to have a more elaborate system of communication than any that has been observed among the gorillas.

Perhaps the most impressive and puzzling feature of chimpanzee life is the chimpanzee "carnival." The natives who live in some regions inhabited by chimpanzees say that occasionally chimpanzees make little clay drums. Then they get together in a large group and while some beat the drums, others jump up and down in a wild dance, and scream and hoot as if they are trying to sing.

That sounds like a tall tale, but it isn't. In 1930, a scientist named Henry Nissen went into the jungle during one of these "carnivals." He was very impressed by what he heard. "Although the cries and drumming presaged no danger to human listeners," he wrote, "their very intensity was sufficient to inspire something akin to excited wonderment . . . when drumming and vocalizing were close by, my guides and porters sometimes trembled in spite of themselves." The "carnival" went on for many hours.

In 1962, the scientists Vernon and Frances Reynolds spent some eight months studying chimpanzees living in the Budongo Forest in the African country of Uganda. During that time the Reynoldses had a chance to see, or rather hear, six chimpanzee "carnivals."

The scientists tried to observe what was going on during these displays, but the chimpanzees were too elusive. They described their futile attempts to watch the "carnival" this way: "Calls were coming from all directions at once and all groups [of chimpanzees] concerned seemed to be moving about rapidly. As we oriented toward the source of one outburst, another came from another direction. Stamping and fast-running feet were heard, sometimes behind, sometimes in front, and howling outbursts and prolonged rolls of drums shaking the ground surprised us every few yards." The scientists found these "carnivals" very memorable and exciting.

What is the reason for all this noisemaking? The Reynoldses believe that the chimpanzee "carnival" is really a means of communication. Gorillas seem to move around in fairly well-ordered and stable groups. But chimpanzees do not live in regular groups. An individual chimp may spend one day with one wandering band of chimps

Dian Fossey (lower left), who is studying gorilla behavior, avoids looking directly at gorilla. Most apes interpret a direct stare as a threat. Photograph by Alan Root © National Geographic Society

and the next with another. Some chimps seem to prefer to be alone most of the time. The Reynoldses speculate that all the chimps over a wide area belong to the same general group, but that this larger tribe is broken up into smaller ones. The members of the tribe do not see one another regularly, but they can keep in touch with the wild noisemaking "carnivals." Just exactly what sort of information—if any—is being communicated by all the loud hooting and drumming, we do not know.

The Reynoldses found that the chimpanzees were the most consistently noisy creatures in the Budongo Forest. A chimpanzee cry could be heard well over two miles away. However, the scientists were never able to get really close to the chimps. Every time the chimpanzees saw humans, they quickly disappeared into the forest.

The first person who was able to get near wild chimpanzees and observe their behavior was a young English girl named Jane Goodall. In 1960, she went to the Gombe Stream Reserve on the eastern shore of Lake Tanganyika in Africa. The Gombe Stream Reserve is the home for about a hundred wild chimpanzees. Jane Goodall endured dangers, illness, and months upon months of disappointment, because for a long time she could go nowhere near the chimpanzees. Finally, her patience paid off and the chimps accepted her, or at least tolerated her as just another creature of the jungle and not something to be especially alarmed about. After she was accepted, Miss Goodall was able to make some of the most remarkable and significant observations of how chimpanzees live in the wild.

Miss Goodall's early observation work was carried on alone. For the first few months her mother accompanied her because local officials thought she was too young to go into the jungle by herself. Her entire staff consisted of one African cook. Later, she was joined by a photographer from the National Geographic Society, which undertook to support her work, and ultimately she married the photographer. Today, she and her husband continue to work at the Gombe Stream Reserve, and they have several assistants.

Up close, the chimps were not nearly as noisy as they had seemed at a distance. In fact, like the gorillas, they vocalized mainly when they were in a highly emotional state. The big difference was that chimpanzees were more emotional than gorillas, and when they did make noise it could be ear-splitting.

A typical example of the chimp's emotional noisemaking took place when Miss Goodall tried to lure the chimps to a new feeding station. In order to observe them more closely, she regularly put out bananas so that the chimpanzees would gather at a particular place to eat. After they had become accustomed to one place, Miss Goodall found a better location for the feeding station. But how were the chimps to be informed of the new location? If they did not find their bananas at the usual place they might simply go away.

She planned to string bananas along the path to the new feeding station, but as things turned out, this was unnecessary. A couple of large male chimps, which Miss Goodall had named David and Goliath, spotted one

75

member of the expedition carrying a whole stalk of ripe bananas. The two chimps were completely overwhelmed by the sight of so many delicious bananas together at one time. They began embracing one another and screaming wildly.

The racket quickly attracted every chimp in the area. Writes Miss Goodall: "We heard wild yells converging from all over the valley. Soon the first of the mob appeared on the steep path, calling hysterically. We scattered bananas liberally on the ground but the chimps, although they gathered them up, seemed too emotional to eat."

Miss Goodall found that chimpanzees behaved much the same way at any time they were very excited. Once she saw a male chimp kill and eat a young baboon. (One of Miss Goodall's most important discoveries was that chimps do eat meat regularly and they will occasionally kill a fairly large animal to get it.) Three other male chimps watched the killing. They embraced one another and screamed, but did nothing else. They did not try to help their companion kill the baboon, nor did they try to steal it from him. This was very strange, because one of the observers was larger and stronger than the chimp that had killed the baboon. Under ordinary circumstances this chimp would have had the pick of any available food. Once again it seemed as though the chimps were completely overcome with emotion, and that the screaming helped to release the emotional tension. The screaming also helped to collect a large crowd. The chimps seemingly were not screaming for the purpose of communication, but communication resulted nevertheless.

The chimpanzees of the Gombe Stream Reserve did not seem to take part in a display quite as spectacular as the chimp "carnivals" of the Budongo Forest, although Miss Goodall did see another noisy and quite mysterious performance. This she called the "rain dance." Chimpanzees do not like getting wet, but during a downpour there is very little they can do about it. Most of the time the chimps just sit around in the rain and look miserable. But sometimes, during a violent rainstorm, one of the large male chimps will begin rushing about wildly, breaking branches off trees and hooting furiously. Other males will join in the "dance," while the young and the females watch. This performance will go on for a half hour or so and then stop just as unexpectedly as it began.

We know that dancing can be a very important means of communication, particularly among primitive peoples. Perhaps our prehuman ancestors took part in rituals similar to those of the chimpanzee "rain dance." Over the centuries, such displays were changed and refined. The various movements and sounds were given meanings. But the chimps do not seem to be trying to say anything with their "dance." It does not "mean" anything to them, as far as we know. They are merely responding to the discomfort or to the stimulation of the pouring rain.

Another situation in which chimpanzees made loud noises is when members of a group that has been traveling together lose sight of one another. Then the male that is leading the group will apparently call the others together with a series of roars or hoots. He may also hit the ground loudly with his hand or with a branch. Whether or not he is consciously attempting to communicate with the members of his scattered band, we do not know.

A chimpanzee that is frustrated, frightened, or angry will also scream loudly. However, the scream of an angry chimp sounds quite different from that of a frightened chimp. These vocalizations are reactions to emotion rather than attempts at communication. However, in effect, they do communicate information about the emotional state of the chimp.

Nowhere is the reaction nature of the chimps' vocalizations shown more clearly than in the actions of a chimpanzee when it is frustrated. Once, Miss Goodall watched a young male chimpanzee she had named Figan spend a morning getting pushed around by the older males in the group. Young chimps are often pushed around by their elders. Sometimes the youngsters react by jumping up and down and screaming. This is not too wise, for such a display may stimulate one of the older males to come over and beat the noisy adolescent. Figan had learned not to make such displays. After he had endured as much pushing around as he could take, he left the group, quietly whimpering to himself. When all alone, and well out of range of the older males, he began hooting loudly and drumming his feet on a tree trunk. After his temper tantrum, Figan was in a better mood and rejoined the group.

Aside from these admittedly loud and spectacular exceptions, the chimps are rather silent. A group of chimpanzees feeding or resting together does not chatter like a flock of birds. Most communication within a chimpanzee group is carried out by gestures, postures, and expressions. A chimpanzee group has a definite social order; certain chimps have the right to boss others around. A low-ranking chimp will approach a higher-ranking one with a particular submissive posture. The low-ranking chimp will be very nervous until the higher one reassures him by a touch of the hand that everything is all right and he has nothing to fear.

Yet chimps are also intelligent and individualistic animals. Their social order is not as rigid as is the social order among other animals that live in groups. A high-ranking chimpanzee may become quite friendly with a particular lower-ranking chimp. Why this happens, we do not know. When his high-ranking friend is around, the lower-ranking animal will boss around chimps who, under other circumstances, outrank him. Some chimps are simply more hostile and bad-tempered than others. Because of the rather loose grouping arrangements, chimpanzees are constantly joining new bands.

Thus, the social world in which the wild chimpanzees live is complicated and always changing. They do not fight out every new social situation to see who should rank top, who second, and so forth. If they did, then

Photograph by Hugo van Lawick © National Geographic Society

Female chimp Melissa (left) extends her hand to adult male Faben, asking him for reassurance. Faben does not react at first, but then, looking grumpy, he begins to soften.

chimpanzees would have to spend all their time fighting one another and they would have become extinct long ago. Most of this very important social information is passed on from one chimp to another by means of gestures, vocalizations, and other signs.

Sometimes chimps communicate with gestures that are startlingly human. When one chimp reassuringly touches the hand of another, this looks very much like a handshake. When two chimpanzee friends that have not seen one another for a while meet, their greeting appears very human. The chimps make little hoots of pleasure as they

Photograph by Hugo van Lawick © National Geographic Society

Finally, reaching out with his palm down, the traditional calming touch, Faben tells her not to worry. Chimps often show extreme nervousness before being reassured by higher ranking individuals.

rush forward and embrace. They will vigorously pat each other on the back. Sometimes they will even "kiss" by pressing their mouth to the other's neck or face.

Jane Goodall was continually impressed by the similarity of chimpanzee and human gestures. She considers this one of her most significant discoveries. There are two possible reasons for the similarities. Either the gestures and postures of man and ape have evolved along parallel lines, or they have a common beginning in the ancient ancestor of both man and ape. Whatever the reason, we can learn a great deal about the way man communicates

81

by studying the way in which chimpanzees and other apes communicate.

Do the chimpanzees inherit their "language" or do they learn it? The study of the behavior of chimpanzees in the wild is just beginning, so we really cannot answer that question with any certainty. It does seem as though they inherit certain basic signs. A chimpanzee born and raised in the zoo will scream in very much the same way that a wild chimpanzee will. An angry zoo chimp shows the same tooth-bearing grimace that the wild chimp displays. But beyond such simple emotional outlets, there is good reason to believe that the chimps do learn a great deal of their "language."

Chimpanzees do not seem to be born with the ability to recognize many of the signs used within the chimp community. As a result, young chimps often commit "social errors," like bothering an angry adult that clearly indicates that he does not want to be bothered. As a result, the young chimps get a goodly number of sound beatings before they learn what others are "saying" to them.

Is it possible that chimps have different languages, just as human beings do? Might the chimpanzees in one place use an entirely different set of sounds and signals than the chimps in another place? We do not know yet.

While Jane Goodall has come to understand a good deal about the language of the chimpanzees, and the chimps have at least learned to tolerate her presence and the presence of her associates, it is doubtful if much communication will ever be established between man and the wild chimpanzees. Since so much of the chimpanzees' language is based on touch, this means that the scientists would have to be in very intimate contact with the chimps to learn it. This could be dangerous because, as we have noted, chimps are very strong and can be unpredictable in their actions.

An even more basic problem is that the job of scientists like Jane Goodall is to observe the natural behavior of wild animals. If the animals being studied were in close contact with their human observers, then their behavior would be changed. They would no longer behave naturally, and the long and painstaking studies would lose much of their meaning.

If man is ever to communicate successfully with chimpanzees or other apes, then these animals have to be brought into man's world.

8

Apes in Civilization

Since ancient times, people have tried to make pets out of apes. None of the attempts have been very successful. An ape can be kept as a captive, but it rarely adjusts to civilization and becomes domesticated as a dog does.

When young, an ape, like a chimpanzee, is playful and appealing. Too playful, in fact, to make a good pet. A young chimp is strong enough and agile enough literally to tear a room apart in a matter of minutes, just for the fun of it.

As a chimp grows older, it becomes less active but more dangerous. An adult male chimpanzee usually weighs at least 150 pounds, but the chimp's arms and hands are more powerful than those of the strongest man. Its teeth would put a large dog to shame. Worst of all, most adult chimps have a sulky, and occasionally downright nasty, disposition. Many adult chimpanzees are offered to zoos by owners who have suddenly been bitten by their once-loving pets. Adult gorillas and, more probably, adult orangutans might have better dispositions, but no one is really sure. They are too rare and much too large to be kept commonly as pets.

Despite all the problems, a few dedicated people have raised apes in their homes in the interest of science.

The most celebrated ape-raising experiment was conducted by Keith and Cathy Hayes. They wanted to see what would happen if a baby chimpanzee were raised like a human baby. Keith Hayes was a scientist working at the Yerkes Primate Laboratory, which specializes in the study of monkeys and apes. (The laboratory was named after Robert Yerkes, a pioneer in the study of primate behavior.) The principal burden of the experiment fell on Cathy Hayes who had a full-time job raising the chimpanzee almost exactly as one would raise a human child. But what a child!

The chimpanzee chosen for the experiment was a female born in the laboratory. She was named Vicki. The chimp was only three days old when she was brought into the Hayes household. Diapered and placed in a crib, the tiny chimp was about as helpless as a three-day-old human infant. But Vicki did not remain helpless for very long.

By the age of four months, Vicki was walking and climbing all over the house. A month earlier she had learned to signal for food by pulling a string.

When Vicki was nine months old she was allowed to share some of her play time with an eighteen-month-old boy. The little ape was more physically developed than the boy. For that reason, she was able to manipulate toys

Young apes are more playful than their elders. Pictured are a young orangutan and a young gorilla.

and tools better. In many respects, the young chimp seemed more curious and inventive—in short, more intelligent—than the human child. In only one area did Vicki fall badly behind. That was the area of language. While the boy could speak about a dozen words, Vicki could not speak at all. Vicki may have actually understood more words than the little boy, for she responded to spoken directions more quickly and accurately, but she could not talk.

Keith and Cathy Hayes were not surprised by Vicki's lack of vocal development. It was obvious, from the time that she was a few weeks old, that speech would be a great problem for the chimpanzee. In her crib the infant ape made a few of the same sounds that a human infant might make. But human infants quickly enlarge the range of sounds they can make. Up until the time they are able to talk, human children spend a lot of time making meaningless sounds. This is called babbling or prattling. With all this noisemaking, the baby is learning, in a playful and random way, how to make the sounds that will become so important to him in later life. Vicki, the chimpanzee, did none of this.

The obvious conclusion was that speech did not come naturally to chimpanzees. This was later confirmed by Jane Goodall, who observed that chimps make noise only when in a state of excitement. Vocalization is not an important part of chimpanzee communication. One of the principal aims of the Hayes experiment was to see if man and ape could communicate. Since Vicki would not learn to speak naturally, as a human does, she would have to be specially trained to speak.

The first task was to get Vicki to produce a sound—any sound—on command. During the training sessions Vicki was first rewarded for every sound she made. Then she was rewarded only for a few sounds, and finally just for one. It was a full five months before she would make a particular noise promptly when signaled. The sound was a strange one, a hoarse "ah," which was different from any normal chimpanzee vocalization.

Next, the scientists wanted to get their young chimpanzee to say the human word mama. This was accomplished by actually manipulating Vicki's lips when she said "ah." Gradually, the couple was able to stop moving Vicki's lips and she mastered the proper lip movement herself. But even after Vicki was able to say mama easily, she continued to put her finger to her upper lip. This was a hang-over from the time that her lips had been moved to form the word. Vicki was fourteen months old before this single word was mastered.

The next few words came more easily, and without lip manipulation. These words were papa, cup, and possibly up. It was not quite certain whether Vicki had mastered the word up or not. At best, the little chimp did not speak clearly.

And that was all she ever said. Years of additional training could not induce Vicki to master one more word.

Vicki was never really comfortable with words anyway. Sometimes she would say "mama" for Cathy, and "papa" for Keith, and "cup" when she wanted a drink of water. But often she did not. She was easily confused and got her words mixed up, or failed to use any words at all.

Everyone who saw Vicki was impressed by her ability to manipulate tools, understand commands, and communicate her desires by non-vocal means. By the age of six she had become so skilled at taking care of herself that she was about to be moved into a little house of her own. It was fitted out with all sorts of gadgets she could operate. Unfortunately, Vicki died of encephalitis before the plan could be carried out. No one knows what Vicki

Infant apes, like this young orangutan, need as much care as human infants.

would have been capable of if she had lived a full chimpanzee life span of twenty to thirty years. No matter how many years she lived, however, she never would have learned to vocalize any better.

Robert Yerkes once said that if a chimpanzee could mimic as well as a parrot, then chimps would be able to talk. But as the Hayes experiment showed, chimpanzees are not good mimics. Even a stupid parrot could have learned a larger number of words than the more intelligent chimp.

These results are rather disappointing. What makes them so is that Vicki can be considered the world's number one, all-time champion talker among chimpanzees.

Several similar experiments have been conducted in the United States and in the Soviet Union. In these, the outcome was even less impressive. One scientist managed to train a young orangutan to say "papa" and "cup," but he had to use the same sort of lip manipulation that had been used on Vicki. There are no good "talkers" in the ape world.

The contrast between noisemaking among apes and birds is great. Many birds make noises almost constantly while awake. Even some mammals—mice, for example—are more "talkative" than apes. Mice do an enormous amount of squealing, squeaking, and chattering. The old saying "quiet as a mouse" couldn't be more wrong. It would be much more accurate to say "quiet as a gorilla." Whether mice use all this noise as part of a system of communication, we do not know for sure, but it is a fairly good bet that they do.

Although a chimpanzee can be very loud, this noise is not part of ordinary chimp communication, any more than loud screams are part of our everyday speech. For this reason, attempts to get apes to imitate "human talk" are probably doomed to failure, as repeated experiments have indicated.

The basic reason why apes will probably never be taught to talk is that they cannot talk—they lack the proper physical equipment to make the sounds that are used in human speech. Dr. Philip H. Lieberman, a linguistics expert and electrical engineer at the University of Connecticut, compared the vocal tracts of apes and monkeys to that of men. Our vocal tract—that is, our mouth and the other portions of our head and throat that are involved in making speech—is very different from the vocal tract of other primates. Behind our nose and mouth is a fairly large cavity called the pharynx. This cavity connects our nose and mouth with our throat, and it also plays an important part in forming the sounds that make up speech. Apes and monkeys have a pharyngeal region that is much smaller than ours.

There are other major differences. The tongue of an ape or monkey cannot move as freely as that of a man, and we must move our tongue constantly when we speak. Vocal cords are also different in structure. The vocal cords of an ape cannot be controlled as well as human vocal cords can. Control of the vocal cords is another necessity for human speech.

Dr. Lieberman thinks that the fossil remains of some of our early ancestors indicate that they could not talk very well either, because they too lacked the proper physical equipment. Although these early men looked human in many respects, their vocal tracts still resembled that of the apes. Man did not learn to speak just because he was smarter than apes. He could make more sounds because he possessed a more highly developed and more useful vocal tract. Man's intelligence then allowed him to use these sounds in a spoken language. Some scientists believe that the development of a spoken language was one of the major differences between man and the apelike creatures that were his ancestors.

By using X-ray movies of newborn infants, Dr. Lieberman determined that the vocal tracts of infants look a lot like those of apes. But at about six weeks of age, the infant's vocal tract begins to change and soon a human baby is capable of producing more sounds than an adult ape.

While an ape's sound-making abilities are very limited, most apes do not make use of the abilities they have. Vicki was trained to make sounds that wild chimpanzees *could* make, but do not. Why apes do not use more sounds, we don't know. For all their intelligence, talking —that is, vocalizing—just does not come naturally to apes. They communicate primarily by other means. As we have seen, gestures are one of the most important ways by which apes usually communicate.

Experiments with chimpanzees have shown that they can imitate human gestures and actions very quickly and very well. You may have noticed a chimp's ability to imitate human actions when you saw one in the zoo. A caged chimp will often mimic the motions of people who are standing in front of its cage. This ability is so well known that it has become part of our language. When we "ape" someone, we imitate what he is doing. Another reflection of the imitative ability of apes and other primates is found in the old saying "Monkey see, monkey do."

Drs. R. Allen and Beatrice T. Gardner, a husband and wife team of psychologists at the University of Nevada, wanted to try a new approach to communicating with

Rarest of all the manlike apes is the pigmy chimpanzee.

chimpanzees. They theorized that communication with a chimpanzee through gestures would be more successful than trying to teach a chimp to vocalize. The Gardners wanted to see if they could teach a chimpanzee sign language. For the project they chose the American Sign Language (abbreviated as the ASL). This is the sign language commonly employed by deaf persons in North America. If you have ever watched deaf persons conversing via sign language, you already know that a great deal of information can be transmitted very quickly by this system.

The ASL contains two different types of signs—representational signs and arbitrary signs. An example of a representational sign is the one for "flower." This sign is made by pressing the fingertips of one hand together and touching them first to one nostril and then to the other as if sniffing a flower. (In the ASL, when all five fingertips are pressed together, they form what is called the "tapered hand.") The ASL sign for "flower" is the sort of sign one might make up during a game of charades, when you have to describe something without using words.

The ASL sign for "always" is arbitrary, rather than representational. It is made by holding the hand in a fist, with an index finger extended (the "pointing hand") while rotating the arm at the elbow. If you did not know American Sign Language, you might guess the sign for "flower" when you saw it, but you probably could never guess the sign for "always."

94

As the subject for their experiment, the Gardners obtained a young female chimpanzee that was caught in the jungle. Because she was born in the wild, the Gardners were not quite sure of her age. They estimated that the chimp was between eight and fourteen months old when she first arrived at their laboratory in Nevada in June, 1966. The chimpanzee was named Washoe, for Washoe County where the University of Nevada is located.

The Gardners did not attempt to raise Washoe entirely in their home as the Hayes couple had done with Vicki. Washoe was kept in a laboratory, though she was not isolated or locked away in a cage all day. For all her waking hours Washoe was provided with human companions. The humans were to act as friends and playmates, as well as providers, protectors, and teachers. An infant chimpanzee can be very demanding, and very tiring, for a single individual, so a regular shift of companions was arranged for Washoe.

At first, the Gardners worried that this constant change of people would upset the little chimpanzee, and prevent her from establishing the sort of trust and affection that would be necessary to make the experiment a success. But Washoe adapted very well and seemed to like all her human companions. The humans became Washoe's family.

In order to make sure that Washoe learned sign language, all the humans who came into contact with her were required to use only sign language in her presence.

The Gardners feared that if the humans both spoke and used sign language to the chimp she might learn to understand speech more quickly. Then, even though she would never be able to repeat the words, she would tend to ignore the signs.

The Gardners also rejected the idea that the humans should talk English to one another and use signs to Washoe. They reported: "Here we reasoned that this would make it seem as though big chimps talk and only little chimps sign [communicate by sign language] which might give signing an undesirable social status."

Of course, the laboratory in which Washoe was being trained was not totally silent. The humans could laugh, groan, clap their hands, and made a variety of other noises. The only rule was that they make noises that the chimpanzee could easily imitate.

Since no one had ever tried to teach a chimpanzee to use sign language before, there were no hard-and-fast rules about how it should be done. The Gardners often had to improvise. They occasionally took advantage of some of Washoe's natural gestures, and then molded them into a rough equivalent of a sign used in the ASL.

Here is how Washoe was taught the sign for "more." Little chimpanzees love to be tickled, and tickling was often used as a reward in order to get Washoe to do something. The Gardners noticed that if they tickled Washoe and then paused, she would take their hand and put it up against the spot that had been tickled. This was clearly signaling that she wanted more tickling. But the problem was not to be able to interpret what the chimpanzee wanted, it was to teach her a sign that could be used in other circumstances.

While she was being tickled, Washoe would always bring her arms together over the place that was being tickled. The ASL sign for "more" is to touch together the tips of the tapered hand repeatedly. Washoe's natural gesture of bringing her arms together was at least a rough approximation of the ASL sign for "more," so the Gardners decided to take advantage of it. When they paused in their tickling, they would pull Washoe's arms away from her body and then threaten to start tickling again. If the chimp put her arms back together again, they would reward her by resuming the tickling.

Washoe was continually shown the proper sign for "more," so that she could imitate it. Often the little chimp's arms were moved into the proper sign. Soon Washoe began to signal that she wanted tickling to start again by putting her fingertips together over her head. This is a very close approximation of the ASL sign for "more," and a great refinement of the original spontaneous gesture of just putting her arms together. The trouble was that the sign did not mean "more," as far as Washoe was concerned; it meant only "more tickling."

The next step was to get Washoe to use the "more" sign in relation to other activities. The little chimp enjoyed being pushed across the floor in a laundry basket almost as much as she enjoyed being tickled. She would be pushed for a while and when the pushing stopped,

Washoe always wanted it to continue. So the experimenter would give the sign for "more." It was not long before Washoe could regularly signal "more" for the laundry basket game. The same procedure was repeated in relation to another of Washoe's favorite games—being swung around by the arms.

After that, Washoe was able to transfer the "more" sign to other activities without being prompted. She was even able to signal "more" when she was still hungry after a meal.

Clever Hans and the other "talking" horses could make signs in response to directions, but when Washoe used the sign for "more," she knew what it meant.

Washoe learned the sign for "open" in much the same way as she had learned the sign for "more." When she wanted to get through a door, she would naturally signal this by pounding on the door with her palms or knuckles. The ASL sign for "open" begins with both hands being held out in front, palms down. The hands are then rotated slowly upwards as they are drawn apart. Washoe had a good start. When she was pounding on a door with her palms, she was standing with her arms out in front, palms down.

If Washoe began pounding on a door she wanted opened, the experimenter would lift her hands off the door and slowly guide them through the motions of the sign for "open." The experimenter also demonstrated the sign for "open," so that she could learn it by imitation as well. In a few months Washoe had learned to use the

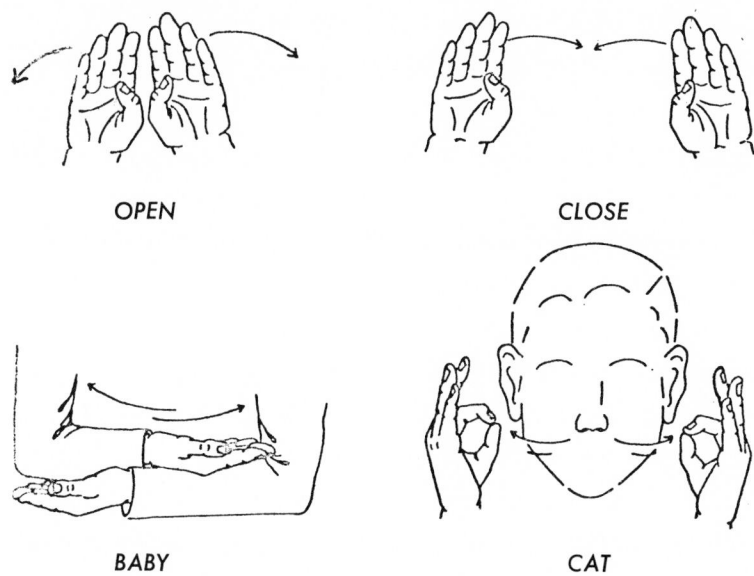

OPEN   CLOSE

BABY   CAT

Signs in the American Sign Language (ASL)

sign reliably to signal "open" for three doors that she used every day. Soon she had transferred the sign to all doors, then to such things as a refrigerator, cupboards, drawers, briefcases, boxes, and jars. One of her own inventions was to use the sign to ask the Gardners to turn on a water faucet.

Some of the gestures that Washoe used naturally resembled those of the ASL so closely that the Gardners hardly had to modify them at all. When Washoe wanted something, she would put her hand out, palm up. This is very similar to the ASL sign for "give me" and "come," so the chimp's natural gesture was incorporated into her language. The outstretched palm is almost a universal sign for "give me" among men and chimpanzees.

99

Another of Washoe's own signs that was incorporated into her language was the sign for "hurry." When she was impatient she would shake her open hand vigorously at the wrist. She might signal to have a door opened, and if it was not done quickly enough, she would shake her hand. This could be translated as "open—hurry." To take advantage of this, the Gardners included Washoe's "hurry" sign into their own sign language in place of the regular ASL sign.

Did Washoe actually know what the sign for "hurry" meant, or was the handshaking simply a gesture of impatience, a reaction to an inner feeling? The Gardners believe that she used the sign in a meaningful way. She used it under different circumstances, for example, when she herself was in a hurry, not only when she wanted someone else to hurry. When she wanted to get to her nursery chair to eat, she would run toward it, shaking her hand.

Every event in Washoe's day was highly ritualized and exaggerated. All the procedures, and all the objects around the little chimp, were named in sign language as often as possible, in the hope that Washoe would understand and repeat the signs by imitation.

Training Washoe took a lot of patience because the experimenters never knew when she was going to imitate an action. Chimps often show what is called delayed imitation. Here is an example: Washoe was bathed regularly; she also played with dolls. But for months she made no connection. Then, one day, during the tenth month of the project, Washoe bathed one of her dolls in the way that she was usually bathed. She filled her little bathtub with water, dunked the doll in the tub, then took it out and dried it with a towel. The entire performance was repeated many times, sometimes with the addition of soaping the doll.

The same sort of delayed imitation took place when Washoe learned the sign for "toothbrush." After every meal Washoe had her teeth brushed. She hated the brushing, but as the months went by, she got used to it. Sometimes she would even brush her own teeth. Every time the toothbrush was brought out it was always accompanied by the appropriate ASL sign for "toothbrush." The sign consists of running the index finger across the front teeth as if it were a brush.

Washoe did not seem to respond to this sign for the longest time. Then, during the tenth month of the experiment, she was in the Gardners' home. She found her way into the bathroom, climbed up on the counter, looked at a mug full of family toothbrushes, and ran her index finger across her front teeth.

The Gardners were elated. They had believed that Washoe understood the sign for toothbrush, but up to that moment they had never seen her use it. They recorded: "She had no reason to ask for a toothbrush because they were well within her reach, and it is most unlikely that she was asking to have her teeth brushed. This was our first observation, and one of the clearest examples of behavior in which Washoe seemed to name an object or event for no obvious motive other than communication."

A major aim of the project was to see if Washoe could transfer the sign for an object or event from one particular object or event to a general class. We have already seen how she transferred the sign for "more" from "more tickling" to "more" anything else; also how she transferred the sign for "open" from "open" a particular door to open a wide variety of doors and other things.

Even more striking was the way in which the little chimp was able to make use of the sign for "flower." Washoe was always interested in flowers. Every time she was shown a flower or taken to a garden where there were a large number of flowers, she was shown the ASL sign for flower. The sign, you may remember, consists of putting the tapered hand first on one nostril and then on the other, as if smelling a flower.

This sign was repeated over and over again for months, but Washoe showed no response. Then one day, during the fifteenth month of the experiment, Washoe was walking with one of her companions toward her favorite flower garden. Quite unexpectedly she touched first one nostril and then the other with the tip of her index finger. It was not quite the ASL sign for "flower" but it was close enough.

After that, Washoe began to use the "flower" sign regularly when shown a wide variety of flowers, indoors and out. She even signaled "flower" when shown a picture of a flower. To make the connection between a real flower and the picture of a flower—which does not smell or feel like a real flower—is a fairly complex bit of thinking, yet Washoe made the connection with surprising ease.

Without being prompted, Washoe began to use her signs in combination to express more complicated ideas. She would stand in front of the refrigerator in which her food was kept and sign first "open" and then "food." At the sound of an alarm clock which signaled her mealtime, Washoe used the signs for "listen" and "eat." These combinations, and others, were her own inventions.

The project with Washoe continues even as this is being written. The Gardners not only want to increase Washoe's vocabulary of signs, they want her to move to a new phase of language. They would like her to learn to answer questions. First, they plan to have Washoe answer simple questions. For example, a box with an object in it will be placed in front of her and she will be asked in sign language, "What is in the box?".

If Washoe masters this sort of simple question, she will go on to more difficult ones like "Where did you go today?". If Washoe can successfully answer questions like that, she will be using much more than the language of reaction, common to many animals. She will be able to "discuss" events that are not immediate. This will imply that she cannot only remember past events, but that she can "think about them."

The Gardners do not know where their experiment with Washoe will end, or what the limits of human-chimpanzee communication can be via sign language. They doubt that they can thoroughly explore the subject in this pioneering experiment. Later experimenters, they believe, will undoubtedly be able to refine and improve their training techniques.

By the time Washoe had reached the age of five she had mastered eighty ASL signs. These she employed in approximately 330 combinations.

Washoe's progress to the age of three was reviewed by scientists from the Salk Institute for Biological Studies. They found that though the little chimp had learned an impressive number of signs, her ability to "talk" was still far below that of a three-year-old human child. Not only that, Washoe used language differently. She rarely talked of the past or future, showed no grasp of grammar and never asked questions or negated propositions. Three-year-old humans do all of these things.

The Salk scientists suspect that "Human language expresses a specifically human way of analyzing our experience of the external world." If this is true, then neither Washoe nor any other chimp will ever really master the human language.

Even so, the results with Washoe are impressive. Everyone has agreed that chimpanzees are intelligent, but previous attempts to communicate with them, by teaching the chimps human speech, had failed dismally because the chimps could not learn to vocalize. The project to teach a chimpanzee sign language may open up a whole new era in human-animal communication.

Another attempt to establish non-vocal communication with a chimpanzee is being carried on by David Premack of the University of California. The subject of the experiment is a seven-year-old chimpanzee named Sarah.

For this project, Premack has devised a series of plastic symbols mounted on metal bases. Sarah quickly learned that a triangle stood for apple, a square for banana, and so forth. It took her longer to learn the meaning of the symbols for such words as "on" and "give." But after intensive training Sarah was able to construct simple "sentences" by sticking the metal-backed symbols onto a magnetized board in a particular order.

When the chimp's trainer, Mary Morgan, gave her an apple, Sarah could describe the event by writing the following "sentence" in symbols: MARY GIVE APPLE SARAH.

After two years, Sarah has mastered 120 words, and some of the other important functions of language. Says Premack, "This does not mean that she can produce all the functions of language, or that she can do everything a human can. But then, we have only been working with her a relatively short while."

9

The Talkative Whales

People once used to talk about "the silent sea." Our ears are not adapted for picking up sounds underwater. Because we could not hear underwater noises, we believed that sea creatures were silent.

Then, men developed different kinds of electronic equipment which could detect underwater sounds. A new world opened up for us, and we were startled to discover that the sea was not at all silent. Quite the contrary; the animals of the sea turned out to be an unusually noisy crew.

Fish grunt and wheeze, and even the clam—fabled for its silence—can make a noise by snapping its shells together. But of all the sea creatures, by far the noisiest are the whales—all of those creatures belonging to the group zoologists call the order Cetacea.

Just about everyone knows that the whales, and the smaller members of the whale family—the dolphins and porpoises—are mammals. Although they superficially resemble fishes, whales are more closely related to the dog, the chimpanzee, and man than they are to the trout or herring. Whales are warm-blooded and they bear their young alive.They do not breathe in the water like a fish does, but must come to the surface regularly to take in air. If a whale cannot get air, it will drown just as surely as any land-living mammal will.

Whales never come onto land naturally; the large whales will suffocate if they are accidentally washed ashore. A whale is so huge that without the water to support its bulk, a whale's chest is crushed by its own weight. A beached whale is unable to breathe because its lungs have been pushed in, but in the sea, whales are the complete masters. They swim farther and faster and dive deeper than any other sea creature.

In recent years, a lot of people—scientists and nonscientists—have become very excited about the possibility of talking to whales, particularly dolphins. This excitement has been generated by two discoveries: First, the discovery that whales are quite intelligent and therefore "worth talking to"; second, the discovery that the whales have a complex language of their own. This language is based on sound, and there is the possibility that we may be able to learn the language of the whale, or that they may be able to learn our language. Let us first look at the problem of the intelligence of whales.

Traditionally, we have believed that the more manlike an animal looked, the more intelligent it was. Therefore, the very manlike apes were considered the most intelligent animals of all. Now, this view has been sharply challenged. Some scientists think that the very unmanlike

107

whales, especially the smaller ones like the dolphins, are at least as intelligent as the apes, and probably a good deal more intelligent.

Those who advocate the intelligence of the whales point out that whales have very large brains. The brain of an adult sperm whale weighs upwards of twenty pounds. The sperm whale has the largest brain of any creature that has ever lived. By comparison, a man's brain is puny, weighing a mere three or four pounds. But, of course, a sperm whale is a lot larger than a man. It may grow to a length of eighty feet and weigh a hundred tons.

A sperm whale is not five or six times as intelligent as a man simply because its brain is five or six times as large. Absolute brain size does not mean anything. Scientists often compare the weight of a creature's brain with its total body weight. This sort of comparison is called a ratio. Here, man comes out on the top of the list for large animals. The ratio of body weight to brain weight in a man is 50 to 1. Yet the creature closest to man on this list is not the chimpanzee or any other ape. The chimp has a body weight to brain weight ratio of about 150 to 1. The animal whose body weight to brain weight ratio is nearest to our own is a small member of the whale family called the bottle-nosed dolphin. The dolphin has a body weight to brain weight ratio of about 90 to 1. (Actually, the dolphin's brain is somewhat larger than that of a man, but the dolphin weighs about twice as much.)

We cannot definitely say that the dolphin is next to

Wild dolphin is captured for transport to Marineland of Florida.

man in intelligence, because the body weight to brain weight ratio is not an infallible guide to animal intelligence. The brains of animals and man are not only of different sizes; they have different structures as well. The brain of a dolphin looks a lot like our own brain, but so too does the brain of a chimpanzee.

We must simply admit that there is still a great deal we do not know about that most complex and marvelous of organs, the brain. The size and shape of an animal's brain may be an indication of its intelligence, but we cannot make any final judgments without a lot of other evidence. What sort of evidence do we have?

Throughout history, sailors and fishermen—who were the only men that regularly came into contact with whales and dolphins—developed a high regard for the intelligence of these creatures. The Greek philosopher and natural scientist, Aristotle, who lived in the fourth century B.C., told a story of how fishermen of the country of Caria caught a young dolphin. Shortly thereafter, a whole group of dolphins came into the harbor and would not leave until the fishermen released their captive. For a long time few scientists would not put much stock in such a story but, in recent years, the cooperative behavior of dolphins has been observed so many times that most scientists would now agree that Aristotle's tale was probably accurate.

At the turn of the century, a famous dolphin named Pelorus Jack regularly met ships that passed through the narrow Cook Strait between the two main islands of New Zealand. The dolphin would lead the way through the treacherous strait, leaping in and out of the water in front of the ship, in full view of the crew and passengers. Jack was rewarded with bits of food tossed from the deck.

From various parts of the world have come stories of fishermen using trained dolphins to help drive fish into their nets. In the sea, dolphins naturally "herd" schools of fish in much the same way that wild wolves will herd reindeer or other animals that live in large groups. So it is probable that these dolphins were not really trained, but that the fishermen made use of what the dolphins did naturally. For their part, the dolphins got a portion of the fisherman's catch.

Dolphins have proved to be enormously popular "zoo animals." One dolphin even became the star of his own television show. The reasons that dolphins are popular are easy to see. Dolphins are very attractive animals; their bodies are sleek and streamlined; they swim gracefully and beautifully; their faces seem to be set in a perpetual good-natured grin; and they can be trained to do such tricks as jump through a hoop or catch a ball.

As impressive as dolphin performances appear, they don't tell us very much about dolphin intelligence. After all, dogs, horses, and even pigs have been trained to perform much more complicated tricks. The repertoire of a performing chimpanzee will put any performing dolphin in the shade. Still, all the people who work with dolphins testify that they are extremely intelligent animals that quickly develop a strong attachment to their human companions.

Since dolphins can now be kept in captivity with relative ease, scientists have had a chance to study them more closely for the first time, but it is still hard to decide how intelligent dolphins really are. It is very difficult to compare the test results of dolphins with those of chimpanzees and men.

Chimpanzees quickly learn to manipulate objects with their hands. In a test, they are able to put a round peg in a round hole, and a square peg in a square hole. We use the same sort of tests for very young children. Because the apes can complete such tests so well, we call them intelligent animals. But a dolphin cannot put a square peg in a square hole because it does not have any hands. The problem involved in setting up tests that will compare the intelligence of land animals that have hands, like man and the apes, with streamlined sea animals like dolphins are enormous. But the dolphin can pull a bell rope with his mouth and push a switch with his nose. It does not need hands for these simple acts.

The results of such tests are not much evidence upon which to base any grand theories about dolphins being more intelligent than chimpanzees, but these are the only hard facts we have. All of the other evidence is subjective—based on the observers' impressions and beliefs. (Subjective evidence is not necessarily wrong or untrustworthy—far from it. It is just a good idea to keep in mind that most of the evidence concerning the intelligence of dolphins is subjective, and therefore open to different interpretations.)

Now let us see how dolphins and other whales communicate with one another.

Most whales roam the seas in large herds. Dolphins often exhibit cooperative behavior, such as getting together to drive a school of fish into a bay or inlet where the fish can be more easily captured, or ganging up on a shark that might be menacing the herd. In order to cooperate, dolphins have to communicate.

The dolphin's face, with its frozen smile, seems immobile. As far as anyone has been able to determine, the dolphin's face does not register expression, like the face of a wolf, a chimpanzee, or a man. With its streamlined body, the dolphin's ability to use gestures also must be

High-leaping dolphins have become popular tourist attractions. Marineland of Florida

extremely limited. Dolphins communicate mainly by sound, just as we do. We cannot properly say that dolphins vocalize, for they have no vocal cords. Yet they produce sounds in a number of different ways.

Sound is vital to dolphins. Not only do they "talk" with it, they also find their way around by sound. The dolphin's eyes are fairly small. (The eyes of the larger whales are so tiny in comparison to their great bulk that on first glance it appears as if they have no eyes at all.) Whales probably do not see too well under water. They navigate mainly by echo location—a system that we call sonar. (Sonar is a word made out of the phrase, sound navigation and ranging.) Submarines also navigate underwater by sonar, but man-made sonar is not nearly as good as the natural sonar of the whales.

While swimming, the dolphin is continually sending out sounds. These sounds are made in air sacs in the animal's head, and apparently are broadcast out into the water in front of the dolphin through its high-domed forehead. When the sounds strike anything in the dolphin's path, they produce an echo. From this echo the dolphin can determine just exactly what is in front of it. Its sonar is sensitive enough to detect a tiny ball bearing dropped into the water fifty feet away.

Dolphins have no external ears as we do. Sound enters the dolphin's head through tiny pinhole-like openings behind its eyes. Inside its head the dolphin has an enormous auditory nerve, much larger than our own. While we do not know exactly how a dolphin hears, we do know that it hears very well.

Many of the sounds that the dolphin makes for echo location are high frequency—that is, beyond our range of hearing. We did not even know that these sounds existed until the development of special electronic equipment that could detect them. (Bats also navigate by means of echo location, and the bats also use high frequency sounds.)

The dolphin makes a whole series of underwater noises —squeaks, clicks, creaks, grunts, groans, hisses, and whistles. It also makes sounds above the water that we can hear. In ancient times fishermen observed that when a dolphin was washed ashore it seemed to groan. They can do a good deal more. Today, performing dolphins are taught to "sing." This "singing" is not very melodic or very loud but it seems to amuse people.

The above-water sounds of the dolphin are made within the animal's blowhole. The blowhole is the dolphin's nostril, but this nostril is on the top of its head. Thus, a dolphin needs merely to brush the surface of the water with the top of his head in order to get a breath of fresh air. It has excellent control over the opening and closing of its blowhole and, for that reason, can make a wide range of sounds by forcing air through it. In effect, the dolphin talks through its nose.

With hydrophones—microphones adapted for picking up underwater sounds—scientists have been able to listen in on the conversation between dolphins. Scientists believe that the whistles, chirps, and tweets made by the dolphins are the sounds used when one dolphin "speaks" to another. The other sounds, like the creakings, are thought to be part of the echo location system.

Numerous examples of dolphin communication have been observed. Scientists aboard the research vessel *Sea Quest* were conducting a study of the California gray whale. The ship was equipped with hydrophones. As a part of the study, the scientists had strung a number of aluminum poles across the entrance to a lagoon that was frequented by the whales, and by dolphins as well. The first creatures to notice the poles were a group of five bottle-nosed dolphins. The hydrophones picked up the dolphins' whistling, which seemed to grow more incessant as they approached the barrier. Finally, the group stopped, and one of the dolphins went forward, apparently as a scout. When he had examined the poles, he returned to his companions. There were a few moments of whistling, and then the dolphins, apparently having decided that the poles were harmless, swam on past them.

In captivity, dolphins that are accustomed to being together in the same pool, and are suddenly separated, will whistle almost constantly for one another. Dolphins that are feeling ill seem to make a particular sort of whistle, while dolphins that come to their aid respond with what might be called a sympathy whistle. Mother dolphins have one sort of whistle with which they call their young, and the young dolphin responds with a different sort of whistle.

One species of whale, the nearly extinct humpback whale, also "sings." Dr. Roger S. Payne of Rockefeller University has spent several years recording the under-

Marineland of Florida

Dolphins on the surface. Note that blowhole on top of head is wide open.

water sounds made by these whales. The sound patterns, which last from five to thirty minutes, have a particular musical quality. They have inspired folk songs, and the recorded sounds themselves have been included in a symphonic composition by Alan Hovhaness called "And God Created Great Whales." Recordings of humpback whale "songs" are being sold and the proceeds used by organizations attempting to preserve the world's dwindling population of whales.

Dr. Payne believes that the humpback whale's "songs" are used for communication, perhaps even long-range communication. "We already know there's a deep sound

117

channel in the ocean," he explains. "This is a layer of water that, for various reasons—temperature, density, and so forth—has acoustical qualities which permit the transmission of sound over very long distances, in some cases more than a thousand miles.

"I'm not saying that whales sit on two sides of the ocean and chat with each other, but it's possible they produce sounds either in or out of the sound channel, which may allow them to flock together. This could take the simple form of 'Humpback whale here!' or maybe even a more sophisticated 'George here!' "

Although still in the early stages of his work, Dr. Payne believes that each whale has a distinctly different "song" and that individual whales can be identified by their "songs."

How extraordinary is this whale "conversation" in the animal world? As we have seen, apes, dogs, and birds are able to signal one another by sound. We have no conclusive proof to indicate that dolphins or other whales communicate more complex information than a pack of wolves or a group of chimpanzees. But the dolphins do have many more sounds at their command than do dogs or chimps. With their large brains and apparently intelligent behavior, most scientists believe that the dolphins do possess a fairly high order of "language."

How much communication has gone on between man and dolphins? In 1964, the zoologist Kenneth Norris trained a bottle-nosed dolphin to respond to a whistle. The dolphin was then released into the open sea, but it always returned to its underwater cage when signaled. People have speculated that one day the dolphins will become "dogs of the sea" and will herd fish for men, just as dogs herd sheep and cattle on land.

Far more intriguing are the possibilities that have been raised by Dr. John Lilly. Dr. Lilly is a medical man whose first interest was human and animal anatomy, particularly the make-up of the brain. He began studying the anatomy of dolphins and was greatly impressed by the creature's huge and complex brain. When he started to work with living dolphins, and found that they learned to push a switch in order to obtain a reward more quickly than a monkey, he became even more fascinated by the animals.

In one experiment, Dr. Lilly placed a microphone over the dolphin's blowhole, in order to amplify the sounds that the dolphin was making. The dolphin seemed to be making noises that resembled human laughter. (There had previously been some laughing going on in the laboratory.) When tape recordings of the dolphin's noises were replayed, Dr. Lilly and his associates made an unexpected discovery. "We discovered that (in a very terse shorthand and quacking sort of way) this dolphin had been mimicking some of the things I had been saying." The dolphin mimicking of human speech—if that is really what these sounds were—has been described as "a very high-pitched Donald Duck quacking-like way."

Perhaps the most startling and almost eerie experience John Lilly has had with the dolphins' ability to mimic

119

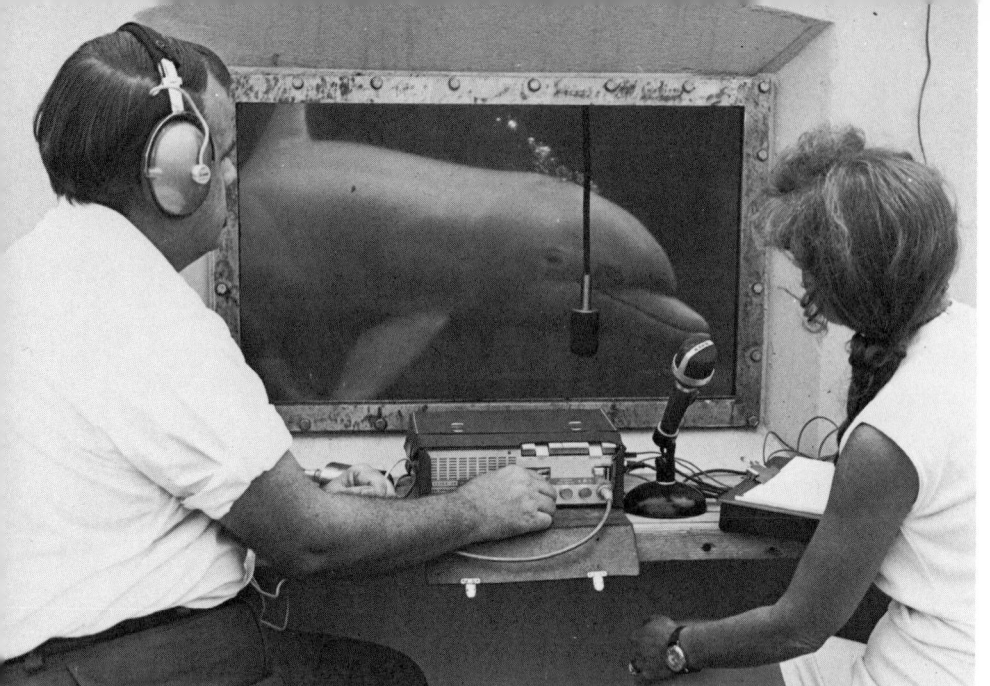

Marine biologist recording the dolphin's underwater sounds

human speech came in 1960. One of the creatures with which Dr. Lilly and his associates had been working became ill. This particular dolphin, named Lizzie, was thought to be one of the most talented at mimicry, and the scientists were very worried about the health of such a valued animal.

One evening Dr. Lilly was standing by the pool in which the sick dolphin was kept. Someone came to him and said that if he did not hurry he would miss dinner. "It's six o'clock!" he was told loudly. A tape recorder picked up this statement and also recorded the noises made shortly afterward by the dolphin. Writes Dr. Lilly: "Lizzie very loudly came out with a 'humanoid' sentence, the meaning of which (if any) has puzzled several of us since. It may have been a poor copy of 'It's six oclock!'

120

But I was caught first by another 'meaning.' It sounded to me like 'This is a trick!' with a peculiar hissing accent. Other people have since heard the tape and come to the same conclusion." The morning after the recording was made Lizzie was found dead.

Dr. Lilly founded the Communication Research Institute in the Virgin Islands. The purpose of this institute is to study the possibility of communication between man and dolphin. Dr. Lilly has received a great deal of publicity. He has often been called "the man who talks to dolphins," but this is a title he has never claimed. What he does believe is that man will be able to communicate

Visual record of dolphin sounds

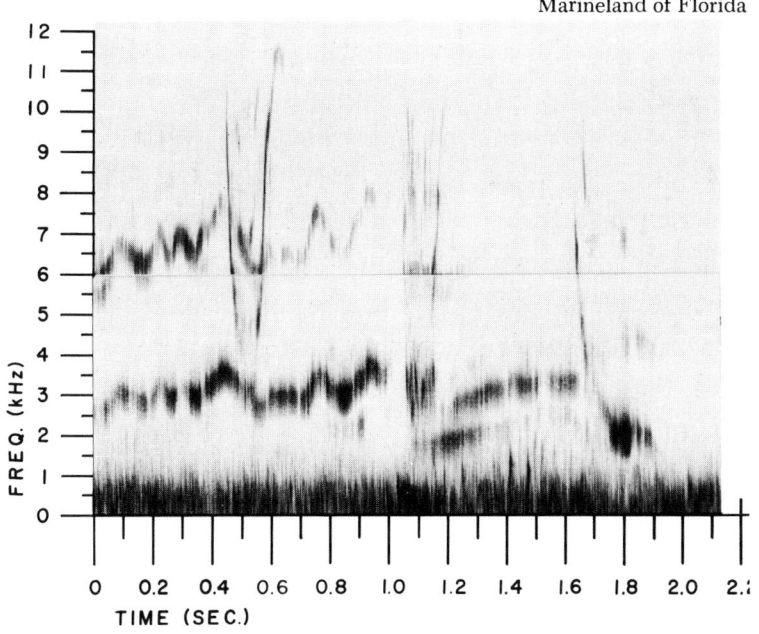

Marineland of Florida

with dolphins in ten or twenty years. He does not say that this communication has taken place yet.

Despite their ability to make a large number of sounds, the dolphins, like Herr Krall's horse, "haven't got a good voice." They have not yet mastered mimicry of human speech. The dolphin is nowhere near the parrot in ability to mimic. Nor has any dolphin even been trained to produce reliably a few simple human words, like the chimpanzee Vicki. John Lilly admits that the few "humanoid" phrases the dolphins do seem to have uttered during the years of research may have been coincidental. But he is not in the least discouraged. He feels that great progress is being made in this frontier area of science.

As an example of progress he cites an experiment conducted in 1965. Two dolphins were being trained to imitate human sounds—not words, but a string of nonsense syllables. Over the several months during which they were tested, the dolphins did not actually learn to imitate the sounds, but they came very close to matching the number of syllables in the sound bursts that they heard. More significantly, the dolphins were not replying with normal dolphin sounds. It seemed to many that they had modified their voices in order to imitate human voices. The dolphins, Dr. Lilly believes, were trying to sound human.

That same year an even more ambitious experiment was carried out at the Communication Research Institute. Margaret Howe, a young employee of the Institute, spent two and a half months literally living twenty-four

A close relative of the bottle-nosed dolphin is the Amazon fresh-water porpoise.

hours a day with a dolphin named Peter. The basic purpose of the experiment was to attempt to bring a human being and a dolphin closer together, to give them a better chance to understand one another.

The experiment was very taxing on Margaret, for dolphins demand a great deal of attention. She stayed next to the pool in which the dolphin was kept, and even slept next to the pool. During the two and a half months, Margaret Howe spent much of her time in the water with Peter Dolphin.

There were no startling results from the experiment, and none had been expected. Margaret gave Peter regular "speech" lessons. Once again, the dolphin seemed to be trying to imitate human words. After a while he would wait patiently for Margaret to finish her sentence, and he would make a noise that may have been an attempt to mimic some of the words he heard Margaret say. In the opinion of many people who have listened to the recordings of these sessions, Peter Dolphin's imitation of human sounds improved during the ten weeks he shared his life with a human companion.

The work of communicating with dolphins goes slowly. We are just learning how to keep dolphins in captivity. Many of them do not live very long after being captured. In addition, man may face problems in trying to communicate with dolphins that he does not face in trying to communicate with dogs or chimpanzees, because dolphins make and hear a lot of sounds that we cannot hear. Perhaps some of these sounds are an impoitant part of their communication system. If so, the dolphins might not be able to communicate properly without using such sounds, nor would the dolphins understand a language that only made use of sounds within the limited human vocal range. Dr. Lilly has speculated that in order to talk properly with dolphins we may need some sort of electronic amplification, with which we could both use and hear high-frequency sounds. We may have to make our own speech and hearing as good as that of the dolphins before we can talk to them.

Practically all communication experiments have been carried out with the bottle-nosed dolphin whose scientific name is *Tursiops truncatus.* The reason is that this dolphin is small—small, that is, for a member of the whale family, although an adult bottle-nosed dolphin can weigh 300 pounds—and relatively easy to capture. But perhaps the bottle-nosed dolphin is not the best subject for a communication attempt. Another small whale (or large dolphin), the killer whale, *(Orcinus orca)* also has a reputation for being extremely intelligent, and it has a larger brain than the bottle-nosed dolphin.

The killer whale has a reputation for being very fierce, but the reputation may be exaggerated. The creature's name is even a bit misleading. Nineteenth-century whalers called this animal the whale killer, because it often attacks and kills giant whales. Somehow, the name got turned around to killer whale, which makes the animal sound a good deal more ferocious. The killer whale is very strong, has lots of teeth, and can be quite dangerous, but many of the stories about killer whales making unprovoked attacks on sailors are simply not true.

In recent years, a few killer whales have been captured and kept briefly in captivity. (They are usually either injured before or during their capture, and die from the injuries or quickly die from disease. We do not know how to care properly for killer whales yet.) In captivity, the notorious killer whale has turned out to be just as friendly and affectionate to human beings as its popular relative, the bottle-nosed dolphin.

Some stories told about killer whales indicate a very high order of intelligence for the creature. One of the most dramatic examples of the intelligence of the killer whales was observed in the middle 1950s. At that time, the Norwegian fishing fleet was plagued by killer whales. Thousands of them surrounded the fishing boats in northern waters. The whales were no danger to the men, but they ate all the fish. In desperation the fishing fleet contacted the whaling fleet and several whaling ships armed with harpoon guns joined the fishermen.

A whaling ship fired a harpoon and struck a killer whale. Within half an hour after this attack, not a single killer whale could be found in the vicinity of a whaling boat. But the killer whales still swarmed around the unarmed fishing boats, even though they looked a great deal like the whaling boats. A message of danger, and a good description of the dangerous ships, was somehow communicated between thousands of individual killer whales over a wide area—and communicated very quickly.

And what are the intellectual capabilities of the great sperm whale whose brain is six times as large as our own? We know almost nothing about sperm whales, except how to hunt them. Hunting whales is something that mankind knows all too well. We have hunted the sperm whale and the other great whales almost to extinction. If we wipe out the sperm whale, we might be missing a magnificent opportunity, because this huge creature may not merely be an intelligent animal, it may actually be more intelligent than man. At least John Lilly thinks so.

Dr. Lilly writes: "Before they are annihilated by man,

Kandu, the killer whale at the Seattle Marine Aquarium. Despite fearsome set of teeth, Kandu was quite friendly.

I would like to exchange ideas with a sperm whale. I am not sure that they would be interested in communicating with me because my brain obviously is so much more limited than theirs. Somehow, I am sure that their huge brain is used effectively. I am also sure that it has capacities beyond my present comprehension."

So, in a way, we have come a full cycle. Primitive men believed that the animals could talk as well as men could, but we simply could not understand their language. They also believed that the animals knew things that we did not know. Finding the key to unlock the secret languages of the animals was thought to be a great prize.

Now, after centuries of regarding the "lower animals" as creatures that could not think, much less talk, we are again looking for the key to the secret languages of the animals. At least a few scientists believe that when and if we find that key, the animals will have a lot to teach us.

Suggested Further Reading

Alpers, A. *Dolphins: The Myth and the Mammal.* Boston: Houghton Mifflin Co., 1961.

Christopher, Milbourne. *Panorama of Magic.* New York: Dover Publications, 1962.

Gilbert, Bil. *How Animals Communicate.* New York: Pantheon Books, 1966.

Harrison, B. *Orang-utan.* London: 1962.

Hayes, Cathy. *The Ape in Our House.* New York: Harper and Brothers, 1951.

Koenig, Lilli. *Studies in Animal Behavior.* New York: Thomas Y. Crowell, 1967.

Lang, Ernst M. *Goma the Gorilla Baby.* New York: Doubleday & Co., 1963.

Lewinsohn, Richard. *Animals, Men, and Myth.* New York: Harper and Brothers, 1954.

Lilly, John C. *Man and Dolphin.* New York: Doubleday & Co., 1961.

———. *TheMind of the Dolphin.* New York: Doubleday & Co., 1967.

Lorenz, Konrad Z. *King Solomon's Ring.* New York: Thomas Y. Crowell, 1952.

———. *Man Meets Dog.* Baltimore, Maryland: Penguin Books, 1953.

Milne, Lorus and Margery. *The Senses of Animals and Men.* New York: Atheneum, 1962.

Reynolds, Vernon. *Budongo, an African Forest and Its Chimpanzees.* New York: The Natural History Press, 1965.

Schaller, George. *The Year of the Gorilla.* Chicago: Univer-
of Chicago Press, 1964.

Tinbergen, Niko. *Animal Behavior.* New York: Time-Life
Books, 1965.

Van Lawick-Goodall, Baroness Jane. *My Friends the Wild
Chimpanzees.* Washington: The National Geographic Society, 1967.

Von Frisch, Karl. *The Dancing Bees.* New York: Harcourt,
Brace and Co., 1955.

Index

131

INDEX

ABOUT THE AUTHOR

DANIEL COHEN is a free-lance science writer and former managing editor of *Science Digest* magazine. His previous books include MYTHS OF THE SPACE AGE, SECRETS FROM ANCIENT GRAVES, THE AGE OF GIANT MAMMALS, MYSTERIOUS PLACES, and A MODERN LOOK AT MONSTERS. His articles have appeared in numerous publications.

Mr. Cohen is a native of Chicago and holds a degree in journalism from the University of Illinois. He lives with his wife, young daughter, two dogs, and a cat in a converted farmhouse near Monticello in upstate New York.